THE WITHDRAWN CANTERBURY TALES

Geoffrey Chaucer

SPARK PUBLISHING

122 Fifth Avenue
New York, NY 10011
www.sparknotes.com

ISBN 978-1-4114-6946-4

Please submit changes or report errors to www.sparknotes.com/errors.

Printed in Canada

10 9 8 7 6 5 4 3 2 1

CONTENTS

CONTEXT

THE CANTERBURY TALES IS THE MOST FAMOUS AND critically acclaimed work of Geoffrey Chaucer, a late-fourteenth-century English poet. Little is known about Chaucer's personal life, and even less about his education, but a number of existing records document his professional life. Chaucer was born in London in the early 1340s, the only son in his family. Chaucer's father, originally a property-owning wine merchant, became tremendously wealthy when he inherited the property of relatives who had died in the Black Death of 1349. He was therefore able to send the young Geoffrey off as a page to the Countess of Ulster, which meant that Geoffrey was not required to follow in his ancestors' footsteps and become a merchant. Eventually, Chaucer began to serve the countess's husband, Prince Lionel, son to King Edward III. For most of his life, Chaucer served in the Hundred Years War between England and France, both as a soldier and, since he was fluent in French and Italian and conversant in Latin and other tongues, as a diplomat. His diplomatic travels brought him twice to Italy, where he might have met Boccaccio, whose writing influenced Chaucer's work, and Petrarch.

In or around 1378, Chaucer began to develop his vision of an English poetry that would be linguistically accessible to all—obedient neither to the court, whose official language was French, nor to the Church, whose official language was Latin. Instead, Chaucer wrote in the vernacular, the English that was spoken in and around London in his day. Undoubtedly, he was influenced by the writings of the Florentines Dante, Petrarch, and Boccaccio, who wrote in the Italian vernacular. Even in England, the practice was becoming increasingly common among poets, although many were still writing in French and Latin.

That the nobles and kings Chaucer served (Richard II until 1399, then Henry IV) were impressed with Chaucer's skills as a negotiator is obvious from the many rewards he received for his service. Money, provisions, higher appointments, and property eventually allowed him to retire on a royal pension. In 1374, the king appointed Chaucer Controller of the Customs of Hides, Skins and Wools in the port of London, which meant that he was a government official who worked with cloth importers. His experience overseeing imported cloths might be why he frequently describes in exquisite detail the garments and fabric that attire his characters. Chaucer held the position at the customhouse for twelve years, after which he left London for Kent, the county in which Canterbury is located. He served as a justice of the peace for Kent, living in debt, and was then appointed Clerk of the Works at various holdings of the king, including Westminster and the Tower of London. After he retired in the early 1390s, he seems to have been working primarily on *The Canterbury Tales,* which he began around 1387. By the time of his retirement, Chaucer had already written a substantial amount of narrative poetry, including the celebrated romance *Troilus and Criseyde.*

Chaucer's personal life is less documented than his professional life. In the late 1360s, he married Philippa Roet, who served Edward III's queen. They had at least two sons together. Philippa was the sister to the mistress of John of Gaunt, the duke of Lancaster. For John of Gaunt, Chaucer wrote one of his first poems, *The Book of the Duchess,* which was a lament for the premature death of John's young wife, Blanche. Whether or not Chaucer had an extramarital affair is a matter of some contention among historians. In a legal document that dates from 1380, a woman named Cecily Chaumpaigne released Chaucer from the accusation of seizing her (raptus), though whether the expression denotes that he raped her, committed adultery with her, or abducted her son is unclear. Chaucer's wife Philippa apparently died in 1387.

Chaucer lived through a time of incredible tension in the English social sphere. The Black Death, which ravaged England during Chaucer's childhood and remained widespread afterward, wiped out an estimated thirty to fifty percent of the population. Consequently, the labor force gained increased leverage and was able to bargain for better wages, which led to resentment from the nobles and propertied classes. These classes received another blow in 1381, when the peasantry, helped by the artisan class, revolted against them. The merchants were also wielding increasing power over the legal establishment, as the Hundred Years War created profit for England and, consequently, appetite for luxury was growing. The merchants capitalized on the demand for luxury goods, and when Chaucer was growing up, London was pretty much run by a merchant oligarchy, which attempted to control both the aristocracy and the lesser artisan classes. Chaucer's political sentiments are unclear, for although *The Canterbury Tales* documents the various social tensions in the manner of the popular genre of estates satire, the narrator refrains from making overt political statements, and what he does say is in no way thought to represent Chaucer's own sentiments.

Chaucer's original plan for *The Canterbury Tales* was for each character to tell four tales, two on the way to Canterbury and two on the way back. But, instead of 120 tales, the text ends after twenty-four tales, and the party is still on its way to Canterbury. Chaucer either planned to revise the structure to cap the work at twenty-four tales, or else left it incomplete when he died on October 25, 1400. Other writers and printers soon recognized *The Canterbury Tales* as a masterful and highly original work. Though Chaucer had been influenced by the great French and Italian writers of his age, works like Boccaccio's *Decameron* were not accessible to most English readers, so the format of *The Canterbury Tales,* and the intense realism of its characters, were virtually unknown to readers in the fourteenth century before Chaucer. William Caxton, England's first printer, published *The Canterbury Tales* in the 1470s, and it continued to enjoy a rich printing history that never truly faded. By the English Renaissance, poetry critic George Puttenham had identified Chaucer as the father of the English literary canon. Chaucer's project to create a literature and poetic language for all classes of society succeeded, and today Chaucer still stands as one of the great shapers of literary narrative and character.

Language in The Canterbury Tales

The Canterbury Tales is written in Middle English, which bears a close visual resemblance to the English written and spoken today. In contrast, Old English (the language of Beowulf, for example) can be read only in modern translation or by students of Old English. Students often read *The Canterbury Tales* in its original language, not only because of the similarity between Chaucer's Middle English and our own, but because the beauty and humor of the poetry—all of its internal and external rhymes, and the sounds it produces—would be lost in translation.

The best way for a beginner to approach Middle English is to read it out loud. When the words are pronounced, it is often much easier to recognize what they mean in modern English. Most Middle English editions of the poem include a short pronunciation guide, which can help the reader to understand the language better. For particularly difficult words or phrases, most editions also include notes in the margin giving the modern versions of the words, along with a full glossary in the back. Several online Chaucer glossaries exist, as well as a number of printed lexicons of Middle English.

THE ORDER OF THE CANTERBURY TALES

The line numbers cited in this SparkNote are based on the line numbers given in *The Riverside Chaucer,* the authoritative edition of Chaucer's works. The line numbering in *The Riverside Chaucer* does not run continuously throughout the entire Canterbury Tales, but it does not restart at the beginning of each tale, either. Instead, the tales are grouped together into *fragments*, and each fragment is numbered as a separate whole.

Nobody knows exactly in what order Chaucer intended to present the tales, or even if he had a specific order in mind for all of them. Eighty-two early manuscripts of the tales survive, and many of them vary considerably in the order in which they present the tales. However, certain sets of tales do seem to belong together in a particular order. For instance, the General Prologue is obviously the beginning, then the narrator explicitly says that the Knight tells the first tale, and that the Miller interrupts and tells the second tale. The introductions, prologues, and epilogues to various tales sometimes include the pilgrims' comments on the tale just finished, and an indication of who tells the next tale. These sections between the tales are called *links*, and they are the best evidence for grouping the tales together into ten fragments. But *The Canterbury Tales* does not include a complete set of links, so the order of the ten fragments is open to question. *The Riverside Chaucer* bases the order of the ten fragments on the order presented in the Ellesmere manuscript, one of the best surviving manuscripts of the tale. Some scholars disagree with the groupings and order of tales followed in *The Riverside Chaucer,* choosing instead to base the order on a combination of the links and the geographical landmarks that the pilgrims pass on the way to Canterbury.

Plot Overview

General Prologue

At the Tabard Inn, a tavern in Southwark, near London, the narrator joins a company of twenty-nine pilgrims. The pilgrims, like the narrator, are traveling to the shrine of the martyr Saint Thomas Becket in Canterbury. The narrator gives a descriptive account of twenty-seven of these pilgrims, including a Knight, Squire, Yeoman, Prioress, Monk, Friar, Merchant, Clerk, Man of Law, Franklin, Haberdasher, Carpenter, Weaver, Dyer, Tapestry-Weaver, Cook, Shipman, Physician, Wife, Parson, Plowman, Miller, Manciple, Reeve, Summoner, Pardoner, and Host. (He does not describe the Second Nun or the Nun's Priest, although both characters appear later in the book.) The Host, whose name, we find out in the Prologue to the Cook's Tale, is Harry Bailey, suggests that the group ride together and entertain one another with stories. He decides that each pilgrim will tell two stories on the way to Canterbury and two on the way back. Whomever he judges to be the best storyteller will receive a meal at Bailey's tavern, courtesy of the other pilgrims. The pilgrims draw lots and determine that the Knight will tell the first tale.

The Knight's Tale

Theseus, duke of Athens, imprisons Arcite and Palamon, two knights from Thebes (another city in ancient Greece). From their prison, the knights see and fall in love with Theseus's sister-in-law, Emelye. Through the intervention of a friend, Arcite is freed, but he is banished from Athens. He returns in disguise and becomes a page in Emelye's chamber. Palamon escapes from prison, and the two meet and fight over Emelye. Theseus apprehends them and arranges a tournament between the two knights and their allies, with Emelye as the prize. Arcite wins, but he is accidentally thrown from his horse and dies. Palamon then marries Emelye.

THE MILLER'S PROLOGUE AND TALE

The Host asks the Monk to tell the next tale, but the drunken Miller interrupts and insists that his tale should be the next. He tells the story of an impoverished student named Nicholas, who persuades his landlord's sexy young wife, Alisoun, to spend the night with him. He convinces his landlord, a carpenter named John, that the second flood is coming, and tricks him into spending the night in a tub hanging from the ceiling of his barn. Absolon, a young parish clerk who is also in love with Alisoun, appears outside the window of the room where Nicholas and Alisoun lie together. When Absolon begs Alisoun for a kiss, she sticks her rear end out the window in the dark and lets him kiss it. Absolon runs and gets a red-hot poker, returns to the window, and asks for another kiss; when Nicholas sticks his bottom out the window and farts, Absolon brands him on the buttocks. Nicholas's cries for water make the carpenter think that the flood has come, so the carpenter cuts the rope connecting his tub to the ceiling, falls down, and breaks his arm.

THE REEVE'S PROLOGUE AND TALE

Because he also does carpentry, the Reeve takes offense at the Miller's tale of a stupid carpenter, and counters with his own tale of a dishonest miller. The Reeve tells the story of two students, John and Alayn, who go to the mill to watch the miller grind their corn, so that he won't have a chance to steal any. But the miller unties their horse, and while they chase it, he steals some of the flour he has just ground for them. By the time the students catch the horse, it is dark, so they spend the night in the miller's house. That night, Alayn seduces the miller's daughter, and John seduces his wife. When the miller wakes up and finds out what has happened, he tries to beat the students. His wife, thinking that her husband is actually one of the students, hits the miller over the head with a staff. The students take back their stolen goods and leave.

THE COOK'S PROLOGUE AND TALE

The Cook particularly enjoys the Reeve's Tale, and offers to tell another funny tale. The tale concerns an apprentice named Perkyn who drinks and dances so much that he is called "Perkyn Reveler." Finally, Perkyn's master decides that he would rather his apprentice leave to revel than stay home and corrupt the other servants. Perkyn arranges to stay with a friend who loves drinking and gambling, and who has a wife who is a prostitute. The tale breaks off, unfinished, after fifty-eight lines.

THE MAN OF LAW'S INTRODUCTION, PROLOGUE, TALE, AND EPILOGUE

The Host reminds his fellow pilgrims to waste no time, because lost time cannot be regained. He asks the Man of Law to tell the next tale. The Man of Law agrees, apologizing that he cannot tell any suitable tale that Chaucer has not already told—Chaucer may be unskilled as a poet, says the Man of Law, but he has told more stories of lovers than Ovid, and he doesn't print tales of incest as John Gower does (Gower was a contemporary of Chaucer). In the Prologue to his tale, the Man of Law laments the miseries of poverty. He then remarks how fortunate merchants are, and says that his tale is one told to him by a merchant.

In the tale, the Muslim sultan of Syria converts his entire sultanate (including himself) to Christianity in order to persuade the emperor of Rome to give him his daughter, Custance, in marriage. The sultan's mother and her attendants remain secretly faithful to Islam. The mother tells her son she wishes to hold a banquet for him and all the Christians. At the banquet, she massacres her son and all the Christians except for Custance, whom she sets adrift in a rudderless ship. After years of floating, Custance runs ashore in Northumberland, where a constable and his wife, Hermengyld, offer her shelter. She converts them to Christianity.

One night, Satan makes a young knight sneak into Hermengyld's chamber and murder Hermengyld. He places the bloody knife next to Custance, who sleeps in the same chamber. When the constable returns home, accompanied by Alla, the king of Northumberland, he finds his slain wife. He tells Alla the story of how Custance was found, and Alla begins to pity the girl. He decides to look more deeply into the murder. Just as the knight who murdered Hermengyld is swearing that Custance is the true murderer, he is struck down and his eyes burst out of his face, proving his guilt to Alla and the crowd. The knight is executed, Alla and many others convert to Christianity, and Custance and Alla marry.

While Alla is away in Scotland, Custance gives birth to a boy named Mauricius. Alla's mother, Donegild, intercepts a letter from

Custance to Alla and substitutes a counterfeit one that claims that the child is disfigured and bewitched. She then intercepts Alla's reply, which claims that the child should be kept and loved no matter how malformed. Donegild substitutes a letter saying that Custance and her son are banished and should be sent away on the same ship on which Custance arrived. Alla returns home, finds out what has happened, and kills Donegild.

After many adventures at sea, including an attempted rape, Custance ends up back in Rome, where she reunites with Alla, who has made a pilgrimage there to atone for killing his mother. She also reunites with her father, the emperor. Alla and Custance return to England, but Alla dies after a year, so Custance returns, once more, to Rome. Mauricius becomes the next Roman emperor.

Following the Man of Law's Tale, the Host asks the Parson to tell the next tale, but the Parson reproaches him for swearing, and they fall to bickering.

THE WIFE OF BATH'S PROLOGUE AND TALE

The Wife of Bath gives a lengthy account of her feelings about marriage. Quoting from the Bible, the Wife argues against those who believe it is wrong to marry more than once, and she explains how she dominated and controlled each of her five husbands. She married her fifth husband, Jankyn, for love instead of money. After the Wife has rambled on for a while, the Friar butts in to complain that she is taking too long, and the Summoner retorts that friars are like flies, always meddling. The Friar promises to tell a tale about a summoner, and the Summoner promises to tell a tale about a friar. The Host cries for everyone to quiet down and allow the Wife to commence her tale.

In her tale, a young knight of King Arthur's court rapes a maiden; to atone for his crime, Arthur's queen sends him on a quest to discover what women want most. An ugly old woman promises the knight that she will tell him the secret if he promises to do whatever she wants for saving his life. He agrees, and she tells him women want control of their husbands and their own lives. They go together to Arthur's queen, and the old woman's answer turns out to be correct. The old woman then tells the knight that he must marry her. When the knight confesses later that he is repulsed by her appearance, she gives him a choice: she can either be ugly and faithful, or beautiful and unfaithful. The knight tells her to make the choice herself, and she rewards him for giving her control of the marriage by rendering herself both beautiful *and* faithful.

THE FRIAR'S PROLOGUE AND TALE

The Friar speaks approvingly of the Wife of Bath's Tale, and offers to lighten things up for the company by telling a funny story about a lecherous summoner. The Summoner does not object, but he promises to pay the Friar back in his own tale. The Friar tells of an archdeacon who carries out the law without mercy, especially to lechers. The archdeacon has a summoner who has a network of spies working for him, to let him know who has been lecherous. The summoner extorts money from those he's sent to summon, charging them more money than he should for penance. He tries to serve a summons on a yeoman who is actually a devil in disguise. After comparing notes on their treachery and extortion, the devil vanishes, but when the summoner tries to prosecute an old wealthy widow unfairly, the widow cries out that the summoner should be taken to hell. The devil follows the woman's instructions and drags the summoner off to hell.

THE SUMMONER'S PROLOGUE AND TALE

The Summoner, furious at the Friar's Tale, asks the company to let him tell the next tale. First, he tells the company that there is little difference between friars and fiends, and that when an angel took a friar down to hell to show him the torments there, the friar asked why there were no friars in hell; the angel then pulled up Satan's tail and 20,000 friars came out of his ass.

In the Summoner's Tale, a friar begs for money from a dying man named Thomas and his wife, who have recently lost their child. The friar shamelessly exploits the couple's misfortunes to extract money from them, so Thomas tells the friar that he is sitting on something that he will bequeath to the friars. The friar reaches for his bequest, and Thomas lets out an enormous fart. The friar complains to the lord of the manor, whose squire promises to divide the fart evenly among all the friars.

THE CLERK'S PROLOGUE AND TALE

The Host asks the Clerk to cheer up and tell a merry tale, and the Clerk agrees to tell a tale by the Italian poet Petrarch. Griselde is a hardworking peasant who marries into the aristocracy. Her husband tests her fortitude in several ways, including pretending to kill her children and divorcing her. He punishes her one final time by forcing her to prepare for his wedding to a new wife. She does all this dutifully, her husband tells her that she has always been and will always be his wife (the divorce was a fraud), and they live happily ever after.

THE MERCHANT'S PROLOGUE, TALE, AND EPILOGUE

The Merchant reflects on the great difference between the patient Griselde of the Clerk's Tale and the horrible shrew he has been married to for the past two months. The Host asks him to tell a story of the evils of marriage, and he complies. Against the advice of his friends, an old knight named January marries May, a beautiful young woman. She is less than impressed by his enthusiastic sexual efforts, and conspires to cheat on him with his squire, Damien. When blind January takes May into his garden to copulate with her, she tells him she wants to eat a pear, and he helps her up into the pear tree, where she has sex with Damien. Pluto, the king of the faeries, restores January's sight, but May, caught in the act, assures him that he must still be blind. The Host prays to God to keep him from marrying a wife like the one the Merchant describes.

THE SQUIRE'S INTRODUCTION AND TALE

The Host calls upon the Squire to say something about his favorite subject, love, and the Squire willingly complies. King Cambyuskan of the Mongol Empire is visited on his birthday by a knight bearing gifts from the king of Arabia and India. He gives Cambyuskan and his daughter Canacee a magic brass horse, a magic mirror, a magic ring that gives Canacee the ability to understand the language of birds, and a sword with the power to cure any wound it creates. She rescues a dying female falcon that narrates how her consort abandoned her for the love of another. The Squire's Tale is either unfinished by Chaucer or is meant to be interrupted by the Franklin, who

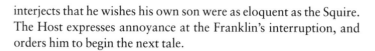

interjects that he wishes his own son were as eloquent as the Squire. The Host expresses annoyance at the Franklin's interruption, and orders him to begin the next tale.

THE FRANKLIN'S PROLOGUE AND TALE

The Franklin says that his tale is a familiar Breton lay, a folk ballad of ancient Brittany. Dorigen, the heroine, awaits the return of her husband, Arveragus, who has gone to England to win honor in feats of arms. She worries that the ship bringing her husband home will wreck itself on the coastal rocks, and she promises Aurelius, a young man who falls in love with her, that she will give her body to him if he clears the rocks from the coast. Aurelius hires a student learned in magic to create the illusion that the rocks have disappeared. Arveragus returns home and tells his wife that she must keep her promise to Aurelius. Aurelius is so impressed by Arveragus's honorable act that he generously absolves her of the promise, and the magician, in turn, generously absolves Aurelius of the money he owes.

THE PHYSICIAN'S TALE

Appius the judge lusts after Virginia, the beautiful daughter of Virginius. Appius persuades a churl named Claudius to declare her his slave, stolen from him by Virginius. Appius declares that Virginius must hand over his daughter to Claudius. Virginius tells his daughter that she must die rather than suffer dishonor, and she virtuously consents to her father's cutting her head off. Appius sentences Virginius to death, but the Roman people, aware of Appius's hijinks, throw him into prison, where he kills himself.

THE PARDONER'S INTRODUCTION, PROLOGUE, AND TALE

The Host is dismayed by the tragic injustice of the Physician's Tale, and asks the Pardoner to tell something merry. The other pilgrims contradict the Host, demanding a moral tale, which the Pardoner agrees to tell after he eats and drinks. The Pardoner tells the company how he cheats people out of their money by preaching that money is the root of all evil. His tale describes three riotous youths who go looking for Death, thinking that they can kill him. An old man tells them that they will find Death under a tree. Instead, they find eight bushels of gold, which they plot to sneak into town under cover of darkness. The youngest goes into town to fetch food and drink, but brings back poison, hoping to have the gold all to himself. His companions kill him to enrich their own shares, then drink the poison and die under the tree. His tale complete, the Pardoner offers to sell the pilgrims pardons, and singles out the Host to come kiss his relics. The Host infuriates the Pardoner by accusing him of fraud, but the Knight persuades the two to kiss and bury their differences.

THE SHIPMAN'S TALE

The Shipman's Tale features a monk who tricks a merchant's wife into having sex with him by borrowing money from the merchant, then giving it to the wife so she can repay her own debt to her husband, in exchange for sexual favors. When the monk sees the merchant next, he tells him that he returned the merchant's money to his wife. The wife realizes she has been duped, but she boldly tells her husband to forgive her debt: she will repay it in bed. The Host praises the Shipman's story, and asks the Prioress for a tale.

THE PRIORESS'S PROLOGUE AND TALE

The Prioress calls on the Virgin Mary to guide her tale. In an Asian city, a Christian school is located at the edge of a Jewish ghetto. An angelic seven-year-old boy, a widow's son, attends the school. He is a devout Christian, and loves to sing *Alma Redemptoris* (Gracious Mother of the Redeemer). Singing the song on his way through the ghetto, some Jews hire a murderer to slit his throat and throw him into a latrine. The Jews refuse to tell the widow where her son is, but he miraculously begins to sing *Alma Redemptoris,* so the Christian people recover his body, and the magistrate orders the murdering Jews to be drawn apart by wild horses and then hanged.

THE PROLOGUE AND TALE OF SIR THOPAS

The Host, after teasing Chaucer the narrator about his appearance, asks him to tell a tale. Chaucer says that he only knows one tale, then launches into a parody of bad poetry—the Tale of Sir Thopas. Sir Thopas rides about looking for an elf-queen to marry until he is confronted by a giant. The narrator's doggerel continues in this vein until the Host can bear no more and interrupts him. Chaucer

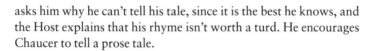

asks him why he can't tell his tale, since it is the best he knows, and the Host explains that his rhyme isn't worth a turd. He encourages Chaucer to tell a prose tale.

THE TALE OF MELIBEE

Chaucer's second tale is the long, moral prose story of Melibee. Melibee's house is raided by his foes, who beat his wife, Prudence, and severely wound his daughter, Sophie, in her feet, hands, ears, nose, and mouth. Prudence advises him not to rashly pursue vengeance on his enemies, and he follows her advice, putting his foes' punishment in her hands. She forgives them for the outrages done to her, in a model of Christian forbearance and forgiveness.

THE MONK'S PROLOGUE AND TALE

The Host wishes that his own wife were as patient as Melibee's, and calls upon the Monk to tell the next tale. First he teases the Monk, pointing out that the Monk is clearly no poor cloisterer. The Monk takes it all in stride and tells a series of tragic falls, in which noble figures are brought low: Lucifer, Adam, Sampson, Hercules, Nebuchadnezzar, Belshazzar, Zenobia, Pedro of Castile, and down through the ages.

THE NUN'S PRIEST'S PROLOGUE, TALE, AND EPILOGUE

After seventeen noble "falls" narrated by the Monk, the Knight interrupts, and the Host calls upon the Nun's Priest to deliver something more lively. The Nun's Priest tells of Chanticleer the Rooster, who is carried off by a flattering fox who tricks him into closing his eyes and displaying his crowing abilities. Chanticleer turns the tables on the fox by persuading him to open his mouth and brag to the barnyard about his feat, upon which Chanticleer falls out of the fox's mouth and escapes. The Host praises the Nun's Priest's Tale, adding that if the Nun's Priest were not in holy orders, he would be as sexually potent as Chanticleer.

THE SECOND NUN'S PROLOGUE AND TALE

In her Prologue, the Second Nun explains that she will tell a saint's life, that of Saint Cecilia, for this saint set an excellent example through her good works and wise teachings. She focuses particularly on the story of Saint Cecilia's martyrdom. Before Cecilia's new husband, Valerian, can take her virginity, she sends him on a pilgrimage to Pope Urban, who converts him to Christianity. An angel visits Valerian, who asks that his brother Tiburce be granted the grace of Christian conversion as well. All three—Cecilia, Tiburce, and Valerian—are put to death by the Romans.

THE CANON'S YEOMAN'S PROLOGUE AND TALE

When the Second Nun's Tale is finished, the company is overtaken by a black-clad Canon and his Yeoman, who have heard of the pilgrims and their tales and wish to participate. The Yeoman brags to the company about how he and the Canon create the illusion that they are alchemists, and the Canon departs in shame at having his secrets discovered. The Yeoman tells a tale of how a canon defrauded a priest by creating the illusion of alchemy using sleight of hand.

THE MANCIPLE'S PROLOGUE AND TALE

The Host pokes fun at the Cook, riding at the back of the company, blind drunk. The Cook is unable to honor the Host's request that he tell a tale, and the Manciple criticizes him for his drunkenness. The Manciple relates the legend of a white crow, taken from the Roman poet Ovid's *Metamorphoses* and one of the tales in *The Arabian Nights*. In it, Phoebus's talking white crow informs him that his wife is cheating on him. Phoebus kills the wife, pulls out the crow's white feathers, and curses it with blackness.

THE PARSON'S PROLOGUE AND TALE

As the company enters a village in the late afternoon, the Host calls upon the Parson to give them a fable. Refusing to tell a fictional story because it would go against the rule set by St. Paul, the Parson delivers a lengthy treatise on the Seven Deadly Sins, instead.

Chaucer's Retraction

Chaucer appeals to readers to credit Jesus Christ as the inspiration for anything in his book that they like, and to attribute what they don't like to his own ignorance and lack of ability. He retracts and prays for forgiveness for all of his works dealing with secular and pagan subjects, asking only to be remembered for what he has written of saints' lives and homilies.

Character List

The Pilgrims

The Narrator The narrator makes it quite clear that he is also a character in his book. Although he is called Chaucer, we should be wary of accepting his words and opinions as Chaucer's own. In the General Prologue, the narrator presents himself as a gregarious and naïve character. Later on, the Host accuses him of being silent and sullen. Because the narrator writes down his impressions of the pilgrims from memory, whom he does and does not like, and what he chooses and chooses not to remember about the characters, tells us as much about the narrator's own prejudices as it does about the characters themselves.

The Knight The first pilgrim Chaucer describes in the General Prologue, and the teller of the first tale. The Knight represents the ideal of a medieval Christian man-at-arms. He has participated in no less than fifteen of the great crusades of his era. Brave, experienced, and prudent, the narrator greatly admires him.

The Wife of Bath Bath is an English town on the Avon River, not the name of this woman's husband. Though she is a seamstress by occupation, she seems to be a professional wife. She has been married five times and had many other affairs in her youth, making her well practiced in the art of love. She presents herself as someone who loves marriage and sex, but, from what we see of her, she also takes pleasure in rich attire, talking, and arguing. She is deaf in one ear and has a gap between her front teeth, which was considered attractive in Chaucer's time. She has traveled on pilgrimages to Jerusalem three times and elsewhere in Europe as well.

The Pardoner Pardoners granted papal indulgences—reprieves from penance in exchange for charitable donations to the Church. Many pardoners, including this one, collected profits for themselves. In fact, Chaucer's Pardoner excels in fraud, carrying a bag full of fake relics—for example, he claims to have the veil of the Virgin Mary. The Pardoner has long, greasy, yellow hair and is beardless. These characteristics were associated with shiftiness and gender ambiguity in Chaucer's time. The Pardoner also has a gift for singing and preaching whenever he finds himself inside a church.

The Miller Stout and brawny, the Miller has a wart on his nose and a big mouth, both literally and figuratively. He threatens the Host's notion of propriety when he drunkenly insists on telling the second tale. Indeed, the Miller seems to enjoy overturning all conventions: he ruins the Host's carefully planned storytelling order; he rips doors off hinges; and he tells a tale that is somewhat blasphemous, ridiculing religious clerks, scholarly clerks, carpenters, and women.

The Prioress Described as modest and quiet, this Prioress (a nun who is head of her convent) aspires to have exquisite taste. Her table manners are dainty, she knows French (though not the French of the court), she dresses well, and she is charitable and compassionate.

The Monk Most monks of the Middle Ages lived in monasteries according to the *Rule of Saint Benedict,* which demanded that they devote their lives to "work and prayer." This Monk cares little for the Rule; his devotion is to hunting and eating. He is large, loud, and well clad in hunting boots and furs.

The Friar Roaming priests with no ties to a monastery, friars were a great object of criticism in Chaucer's time. Always ready to befriend young women or rich men who might need his services, the friar actively administers the sacraments in his town, especially those of marriage and confession. However, Chaucer's worldly Friar has taken to accepting bribes.

The Summoner The Summoner brings persons accused of violating Church law to ecclesiastical court. This Summoner is a lecherous man whose face is scarred by leprosy. He gets drunk frequently, is irritable, and is not particularly qualified for his position. He spouts the few words of Latin he knows in an attempt to sound educated.

The Host The leader of the group, the Host is large, loud, and merry, although he possesses a quick temper. He mediates among the pilgrims and facilitates the flow of the tales. His title of "host" may be a pun, suggesting both an innkeeper and the Eucharist, or Holy Host.

The Parson The only devout churchman in the company, the Parson lives in poverty, but is rich in holy thoughts and deeds. The pastor of a sizable town, he preaches the Gospel and makes sure to practice what he preaches. He is everything that the Monk, the Friar, and the Pardoner are not.

The Squire The Knight's son and apprentice. The Squire is curly-haired, youthfully handsome, and loves dancing and courting.

The Clerk The Clerk is a poor student of philosophy. Having spent his money on books and learning rather than on fine clothes, he is threadbare and wan. He speaks little, but when he does, his words are wise and full of moral virtue.

The Man of Law A successful lawyer commissioned by the king. He upholds justice in matters large and small and knows every statute of England's law by heart.

The Manciple A manciple was in charge of getting provisions for a college or court. Despite his lack of education, this Manciple is smarter than the thirty lawyers he feeds.

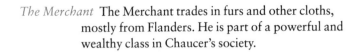

The Merchant The Merchant trades in furs and other cloths, mostly from Flanders. He is part of a powerful and wealthy class in Chaucer's society.

The Shipman Brown-skinned from years of sailing, the Shipman has seen every bay and river in England, and exotic ports in Spain and Carthage as well. He is a bit of a rascal, known for stealing wine while the ship's captain sleeps.

The Physician The Physician is one of the best in his profession, for he knows the cause of every malady and can cure most of them. Though the Physician keeps himself in perfect physical health, the narrator calls into question the Physician's spiritual health: he rarely consults the Bible and has an unhealthy love of financial gain.

The Franklin The word "franklin" means "free man." In Chaucer's society, a franklin was neither a vassal serving a lord nor a member of the nobility. This particular franklin is a connoisseur of food and wine, so much so that his table remains laid and ready for food all day.

The Reeve A reeve was similar to a steward of a manor, and this reeve performs his job shrewdly—his lord never loses so much as a ram to the other employees, and the vassals under his command are kept in line. However, he steals from his master.

The Plowman The Plowman is the Parson's brother and is equally good-hearted. A member of the peasant class, he pays his tithes to the Church and leads a good Christian life.

The Guildsmen Listed together, the five Guildsmen appear as a unit. English guilds were a combination of labor unions and social fraternities: craftsmen of similar occupations joined together to increase their bargaining power and live communally. All five Guildsmen are clad in the livery of their brotherhood.

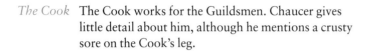

The Cook The Cook works for the Guildsmen. Chaucer gives little detail about him, although he mentions a crusty sore on the Cook's leg.

The Yeoman The servant who accompanies the Knight and the Squire. The narrator mentions that his dress and weapons suggest he may be a forester.

The Second Nun The Second Nun is not described in the General Prologue, but she tells of a saint's life for her tale.

The Nun's Priest Like the Second Nun, the Nun's Priest is not described in the General Prologue. His story of Chanticleer, however, is well crafted and suggests that he is a witty, self-effacing preacher.

CHARACTERS FROM THE FIVE TALES ANALYZED IN THIS SPARKNOTE

THE KNIGHT'S TALE

Theseus A great conqueror and the duke of Athens in the Knight's Tale. The most powerful ruler in the story, he is often called upon to make the final judgment, but he listens to others' pleas for help.

Palamon Palamon is one of the two imprisoned Theban soldier heroes in the Knight's Tale. Brave, strong, and sworn to everlasting friendship with his cousin Arcite, Palamon falls in love with the fair maiden Emelye, which brings him into conflict with Arcite. Though he loses the tournament against Arcite, he gets Emelye in the end.

Arcite The sworn brother to Palamon, Arcite, imprisoned with Palamon in the tower in the Knight's Tale, falls equally head over heels in love with Emelye. He gets released from the tower early and wins Emelye's hand in a tournament, but then dies when a divinely fated earthquake causes his horse to throw him.

Emelye   Emelye is the sister to Hippolyta, Theseus's domesticated Amazon queen in the Knight's Tale. Fair-haired and glowing, we first see Emelye as Palamon does, through a window. Although she is the object of both Palamon's and Arcite's desire, she would rather spend her life unmarried and childless. Nevertheless, when Arcite wins the tournament, she readily pledges herself to him.

Egeus   Theseus's father. Egeus gives Theseus the advice that helps him convince Palamon and Emelye to end their mourning of Arcite and get married.

The Miller's Tale

Nicholas   In the Miller's Tale, Nicholas is a poor astronomy student who boards with an elderly carpenter, John, and the carpenter's too-young wife, Alisoun. Nicholas dupes John and sleeps with Alisoun right under John's nose, but Absolon, the foppish parish clerk, gets Nicholas in the end.

Alisoun   Alisoun is the sexy young woman married to the carpenter in the Miller's Tale. She is bright and sweet like a small bird, and dresses in a tantalizing style—her clothes are embroidered inside and outside, and she laces her boots high. She willingly goes to bed with Nicholas, but she has only harsh words and obscenities for Absolon.

Absolon   The local parish clerk in the Miller's Tale, Absolon is a little bit foolish and more than a little bit vain. He wears red stockings underneath his floor-length church gown, and his leather shoes are decorated like the fanciful stained-glass windows in a cathedral. He curls his hair, uses breath fresheners, and fancies Alisoun.

John   The dim-witted carpenter to whom Alisoun is married and with whom Nicholas boards. John is jealous and possessive of his wife. He constantly berates Nicholas for looking into God's "pryvetee," but when Nicholas offers John the chance to share his knowledge, John quickly accepts. He gullibly believes Nicholas's pronouncement that a second flood is coming, which allows Nicholas to sleep with John's wife.

THE WIFE OF BATH'S PROLOGUE AND TALE

The First Three Husbands The Wife of Bath says that her first three husbands were "good" because they were rich and old. She could order them around, use sex to get what she wanted, and trick them into believing lies.

The Fourth Husband The Wife of Bath says comparatively little about her fourth husband. She loved him, but he was a reveler who had a mistress. She had fun singing and dancing with him, but tried her best to make him jealous. She fell in love with her fifth husband, Jankyn, while she was still married to her fourth.

Jankyn The Wife of Bath's fifth husband, Jankyn, was a twenty-year-old former student, with whom the Wife was madly in love. His stories of wicked wives frustrated her so much that one night she ripped a page out of his book, only to receive a deafening smack on her ear in return.

The Knight Arthur's young knight rapes a maiden, and, to avoid the punishment of death, he is sent by the queen on a quest to learn about submission to women. Once he does so, and shows that he has learned his lesson by letting his old ugly wife make a decision, she rewards him by becoming beautiful and submissive.

The Old Woman The old woman supplies the young knight with the answer to his question, in exchange for his promise to do whatever she wants. When she tells him he must marry her, the knight begrudgingly agrees, and when he allows her to choose whether she would like to be beautiful and unfaithful or ugly and faithful, she rewards him by becoming both beautiful and faithful.

Arthur's Queen Arthur's queen, presumably Guinevere, is interesting because she wields most of the power. When Arthur's knight rapes a maiden, he turns the knight over to his queen allows her to decide what to do with him.

THE PARDONER'S TALE

The Three Rioters These are the three protagonists of the Pardoner's Tale. All three indulge in and represent the vices against which the Pardoner has railed in his Prologue: Gluttony, Drunkeness, Gambling, and Swearing. These traits define the three and eventually lead to their downfall. The Rioters at first appear like personified vices, but it is their belief that a personified concept—in this case, Death—is a real person that becomes the root cause of their undoing.

The Old Man In the Pardoner's Tale, the three Rioters encounter a very old man whose body is completely covered except for his face. Before the old man tells the Rioters where they can find "Death," one of the Rioters rashly demands why the old man is still alive. The old man answers that he is doomed to walk the earth for eternity. He has been interpreted as Death itself, or as Cain, punished for fratricide by walking the earth forever; or as the Wandering Jew, a man who refused to let Christ rest at his house when Christ proceeded to his crucifixion, and who was therefore doomed to roam the world, through the ages, never finding rest.

THE NUN'S PRIEST'S TALE

Chanticleer The heroic rooster of the Nun's Priest's Tale, Chanticleer has seven hen-wives and is the most handsome cock in the barnyard. One day, he has a prophetic dream of a fox that will carry him away. Chanticleer is also a bit vain about his clear and accurate crowing voice, and he unwittingly allows a fox to flatter him out of his liberty.

Pertelote	Chanticleer's favorite wife in the Nun's Priest's Tale. She is his equal in looks, manners, and talent. When Chanticleer dreams of the fox, he awakens her in the middle of the night, begging for an interpretation, but Pertelote will have none of it, calling him foolish. When the fox takes him away, she mourns him in classical Greek fashion, burning herself and wailing.
The Fox	The orange fox, interpreted by some as an allegorical figure for the devil, catches Chanticleer the rooster through flattery. Eventually, Chanticleer outwits the fox by encouraging him to boast of his deceit to his pursuers. When the fox opens his mouth, Chanticleer escapes.

ANALYSIS OF MAJOR CHARACTERS

THE KNIGHT

The Knight rides at the front of the procession described in the General Prologue, and his story is the first in the sequence. The Host clearly admires the Knight, as does the narrator. The narrator seems to remember four main qualities of the Knight. The first is the Knight's love of ideals—"chivalrie" (prowess), "trouthe" (fidelity), "honour" (reputation), "fredom" (generosity), and "curteisie" (refinement) (General Prologue, 45–46). The second is the Knight's impressive military career. The Knight has fought in the Crusades, wars in which Europeans traveled by sea to non-Christian lands and attempted to convert whole cultures by the force of their swords. By Chaucer's time, the spirit for conducting these wars was dying out, and they were no longer undertaken as frequently. The Knight has battled the Muslims in Egypt, Spain, and Turkey, and the Russian Orthodox in Lithuania and Russia. He has also fought in formal duels. The third quality the narrator remembers about the Knight is his meek, gentle, manner. And the fourth is his "array," or dress. The Knight wears a tunic made of coarse cloth, and his coat of mail is rust-stained, because he has recently returned from an expedition.

The Knight's interaction with other characters tells us a few additional facts about him. In the Prologue to the Nun's Priest's Tale, he calls out to hear something more lighthearted, saying that it deeply upsets him to hear stories about tragic falls. He would rather hear about "joye and greet solas," about men who start off in poverty climbing in fortune and attaining wealth (Nun's Priest's Prologue, 2774). The Host agrees with him, which is not surprising, since the Host has mentioned that whoever tells the tale of "best sentence and moost solaas" will win the storytelling contest (General Prologue, 798). And, at the end of the Pardoner's Tale, the Knight breaks in to stop the squabbling between the Host and the Pardoner, ordering them to kiss and make up. Ironically, though a soldier, the romantic, idealistic Knight clearly has an aversion to conflict or unhappiness of any sort.

THE PARDONER

The Pardoner rides in the very back of the party in the General Prologue and is fittingly the most marginalized character in the company. His profession is somewhat dubious—pardoners offered indulgences, or previously written pardons for particular sins, to people who repented of the sin they had committed. Along with receiving the indulgence, the penitent would make a donation to the Church by giving money to the pardoner. Eventually, this "charitable" donation became a necessary part of receiving an indulgence. Paid by the Church to offer these indulgences, the Pardoner was not supposed to pocket the penitents' charitable donations. That said, the practice of offering indulgences came under critique by quite a few churchmen, since once the charitable donation became a practice allied to receiving an indulgence, it began to look like one could cleanse oneself of sin by simply paying off the Church. Additionally, widespread suspicion held that pardoners counterfeited the pope's signature on illegitimate indulgences and pocketed the "charitable donations" themselves.

Chaucer's Pardoner is a highly untrustworthy character. He sings a ballad—"Com hider, love, to me!" (General Prologue, 672)—with the hypocritical Summoner, undermining the already challenged virtue of his profession as one who works for the Church. He presents himself as someone of ambiguous gender and sexual orientation, further challenging social norms. The narrator is not sure whether the Pardoner is an effeminate homosexual or a eunuch (castrated male). Like the other pilgrims, the Pardoner carries with him to Canterbury the tools of his trade—in his case, freshly signed papal indulgences and a sack of false relics, including a brass cross filled with stones to make it seem as heavy as gold and a glass jar full of pig's bones, which he passes off as saints' relics. Since visiting relics on pilgrimage had become a tourist industry, the Pardoner wants to cash in on religion in any way he can, and he does this by selling tangible, material objects—whether slips of paper that promise forgiveness of sins or animal bones that people can string around their necks as charms against the devil. After telling the group how he gulls people into indulging his own avarice through a sermon he preaches on greed, the Pardoner tells a tale that exemplifies the vice decried in his sermon. Furthermore, he attempts to sell pardons to the group—in effect plying his trade in clear violation of the rules outlined by the host.

THE WIFE OF BATH

One of two female storytellers (the other is the Prioress), the Wife has a lot of experience under her belt. She has traveled all over the world on pilgrimages, so Canterbury is a jaunt compared to other perilous journeys she has endured. Not only has she seen many lands, she has lived with five husbands. She is worldly in both senses of the word: she has seen the world and has experience in the ways of the world, that is, in love and sex.

Rich and tasteful, the Wife's clothes veer a bit toward extravagance: her face is wreathed in heavy cloth, her stockings are a fine scarlet color, and the leather on her shoes is soft, fresh, and brand new—all of which demonstrate how wealthy she has become. Scarlet was a particularly costly dye, since it was made from individual red beetles found only in some parts of the world. The fact that she hails from Bath, a major English cloth-making town in the Middle Ages, is reflected in both her talent as a seamstress and her stylish garments. Bath at this time was fighting for a place among the great European exporters of cloth, which were mostly in the Netherlands and Belgium. So the fact that the Wife's sewing surpasses that of the cloth makers of "Ipres and of Gaunt" (Ypres and Ghent) speaks well of Bath's (and England's) attempt to outdo its overseas competitors.

Although she is argumentative and enjoys talking, the Wife is intelligent in a commonsense, rather than intellectual, way. Through her experiences with her husbands, she has learned how to provide for herself in a world where women had little independence or power. The chief manner in which she has gained control over her husbands has been in her control over their use of her body. The Wife uses her body as a bargaining tool, withholding sexual pleasure until her husbands give her what she demands.

Themes, Motifs & Symbols

Themes

Themes are the fundamental and often universal ideas explored in a literary work.

The Pervasiveness of Courtly Love

The phrase "courtly love" refers to a set of ideas about love that was enormously influential on the literature and culture of the Middle Ages. Beginning with the Troubadour poets of southern France in the eleventh century, poets throughout Europe promoted the notions that true love only exists outside of marriage; that true love may be idealized and spiritual, and may exist without ever being physically consummated; and that a man becomes the servant of the lady he loves. Together with these basic premises, courtly love encompassed a number of minor motifs. One of these is the idea that love is a torment or a disease, and that when a man is in love he cannot sleep or eat, and therefore he undergoes physical changes, sometimes to the point of becoming unrecognizable. Although very few people's lives resembled the courtly love ideal in any way, these themes and motifs were extremely popular and widespread in medieval and Renaissance literature and culture. They were particularly popular in the literature and culture that were part of royal and noble courts.

Courtly love motifs first appear in *The Canterbury Tales* with the description of the Squire in the General Prologue. The Squire's role in society is exactly that of his father the Knight, except for his lower status, but the Squire is very different from his father in that he incorporates the ideals of courtly love into his interpretation of his own role. Indeed, the Squire is practically a parody of the traditional courtly lover. The description of the Squire establishes a pattern that runs throughout the General Prologue, and *The Canterbury Tales*: characters whose roles are defined by their religious or economic functions integrate the cultural ideals of courtly love into their dress, their behavior, and the tales they tell, in order to give a slightly different twist to their roles. Another such character is the Prioress, a nun who sports a "Love Conquers All" brooch.

THE IMPORTANCE OF COMPANY

Many of Chaucer's characters end their stories by wishing the rest of the "compaignye," or company, well. The Knight ends with "God save al this faire compaignye" (3108), and the Reeve with "God, that sitteth heighe in magestee, / Save al this compaignye, grete and smale!" (4322–4323). Company literally signifies the entire group of people, but Chaucer's deliberate choice of this word over other words for describing masses of people, like the Middle English words for party, mixture, or group, points us to another major theme that runs throughout *The Canterbury Tales*. Company derives from two Latin words, *com,* or "with," and *pane,* or "bread." Quite literally, a company is a group of people with whom one eats, or breaks bread. The word for good friend, or "companion," also comes from these words. But, in a more abstract sense, company had an economic connotation. It was the term designated to connote a group of people engaged in a particular business, as it is used today.

The functioning and well-being of medieval communities, not to mention their overall happiness, depended upon groups of socially bonded workers in towns and guilds, known informally as companies. If workers in a guild or on a feudal manor were not getting along well, they would not produce good work, and the economy would suffer. They would be unable to bargain, as a modern union does, for better working conditions and life benefits. Eating together was a way for guild members to cement friendships, creating a support structure for their working community. Guilds had their own special dining halls, where social groups got together to bond, be merry, and form supportive alliances. When the peasants revolted against their feudal lords in 1381, they were able to organize themselves well precisely because they had formed these strong social ties through their companies.

Company was a leveling concept—an idea created by the working classes that gave them more power and took away some of the nobility's power and tyranny. The company of pilgrims on the way to Canterbury is not a typical example of a tightly networked company, although the five Guildsmen do represent this kind of fraternal union. The pilgrims come from different parts of society—the court, the Church, villages, the feudal manor system. To prevent discord, the pilgrims create an informal company, united by their jobs as storytellers, and by the food and drink the host provides. As far as class distinctions are concerned, they do form a company in the sense that none of them belongs to the nobility, and most have working professions, whether that work be sewing and marriage (the Wife of Bath), entertaining visitors with gourmet food (the Franklin), or tilling the earth (the Plowman).

THE CORRUPTION OF THE CHURCH

By the late fourteenth century, the Catholic Church, which governed England, Ireland, and the entire continent of Europe, had become extremely wealthy. The cathedrals that grew up around shrines to saints' relics were incredibly expensive to build, and the amount of gold that went into decorating them and equipping them with candlesticks and reliquaries (boxes to hold relics that were more jewel-encrusted than kings' crowns) surpassed the riches in the nobles' coffers. In a century of disease, plague, famine, and scarce labor, the sight of a church ornamented with unused gold seemed unfair to some people, and the Church's preaching against greed suddenly seemed hypocritical, considering its great displays of material wealth. Distaste for the excesses of the Church triggered stories and anecdotes about greedy, irreligious churchmen who accepted bribes, bribed others, and indulged themselves sensually and gastronomically, while ignoring the poor famished peasants begging at their doors.

The religious figures Chaucer represents in *The Canterbury Tales* all deviate in one way or another from what was traditionally expected of them. Generally, their conduct corresponds to common medieval stereotypes, but it is difficult to make any overall statement about Chaucer's position because his narrator is so clearly biased toward some characters—the Monk, for example—and so clearly biased against others, such as the Pardoner. Additionally, the characters are not simply satirical versions of their roles; they are individuals and cannot simply be taken as typical of their professions.

The Monk, Prioress, and Friar were all members of the clerical estate. The Monk and the Prioress live in a monastery and a convent, respectively. Both are characterized as figures who seem to prefer the aristocratic to the devotional life. The Prioress's bejeweled rosary seems more like a love token than something expressing her devotion to Christ, and her dainty mannerisms echo the advice given by Guillaume de Loris in the French romance *Roman de la Rose,* about how women could make themselves attractive to men. The Monk enjoys hunting, a pastime of the nobility, while he disdains study and confinement. The Friar was a member of an order of mendicants, who made their living by traveling around and begging, and accepting money to hear confession. Friars were often seen as threatening and had the reputation of being lecherous, as the Wife of Bath describes in the opening of her tale. The Summoner and the Friar are at each other's throats so frequently in *The Canterbury Tales* because they were in fierce competition in Chaucer's time—summoners, too, extorted money from people.

Overall, the narrator seems to harbor much more hostility for the ecclesiastical officials (the Summoner and the Pardoner) than he does for the clerics. For example, the Monk and the Pardoner possess several traits in common, but the narrator presents them in very different ways. The narrator remembers the shiny baldness of the Monk's head, which suggests that the Monk may have ridden without a hood, but the narrator uses the fact that the Pardoner rides without a hood as proof of his shallow character. The Monk and the Pardoner both give their own opinions of themselves to the narrator—the narrator affirms the Monk's words by repeating them, and his own response, but the narrator mocks the Pardoner for his opinion of himself.

MOTIFS

Motifs are recurring structures, contrasts, and literary devices that can help to develop and inform the text's major themes.

ROMANCE

The romance, a tale about knights and ladies incorporating courtly love themes, was a popular literary genre in fourteenth-century literature. The genre included tales of knights rescuing maidens, embarking on quests, and forming bonds with other knights and rulers (kings and queens). In particular, the romances about King Arthur, his queen, Guinevere, and his society of "knights of the round table" were very popular in England. In *The Canterbury Tales,* the Knight's Tale incorporates romantic elements in an ancient classical setting, which is a somewhat unusual time and place to set a romance. The Wife of Bath's Tale is framed by Arthurian romance, with an unnamed knight of the round table as its unlikely hero, but the tale itself becomes a proto-feminist's moral instruction for domestic behavior. The Miller's Tale ridicules the traditional elements

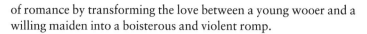

of romance by transforming the love between a young wooer and a willing maiden into a boisterous and violent romp.

FABLIAUX

Fabliaux were comical and often grotesque stories in which the characters most often succeed by means of their sharp wits. Such stories were popular in France and Italy in the fourteenth century. Frequently, the plot turns or climaxes around the most grotesque feature in the story, usually a bodily noise or function. The Miller's Tale is a prime experiment with this motif: Nicholas cleverly tricks the carpenter into spending the night in his barn so that Nicholas can sleep with the carpenter's wife; the finale occurs when Nicholas farts in Absolon's face, only to be burned with a hot poker on his rear end. In the Summoner's Tale, a wealthy man bequeaths a corrupt friar an enormous fart, which the friar divides twelve ways among his brethren. This demonstrates another invention around this motif—that of wittily expanding a grotesque image in an unconventional way. In the case of the Summoner's Tale, the image is of flatulence, but the tale excels in discussing the division of the fart in a highly intellectual (and quite hilarious) manner.

SYMBOLS

Symbols are objects, characters, figures, and colors used to represent abstract ideas or concepts.

SPRINGTIME

The Canterbury Tales opens in April, at the height of spring. The birds are chirping, the flowers blossoming, and people long in their hearts to go on pilgrimages, which combine travel, vacation, and spiritual renewal. The springtime symbolizes rebirth and fresh beginnings, and is thus appropriate for the beginning of Chaucer's text. Springtime also evokes erotic love, as evidenced by the moment when Palamon first sees Emelye gathering fresh flowers to make garlands in honor of May. The Squire, too, participates in this symbolism. His devotion to courtly love is compared to the freshness of the month of May.

CLOTHING

In the General Prologue, the description of garments, in addition to the narrator's own shaky recollections, helps to define each character. In a sense, the clothes symbolize what lies beneath the surface of each personality. The Physician's love of wealth reveals itself most clearly to us in the rich silk and fur of his gown. The Squire's youthful vanity is symbolized by the excessive floral brocade on his tunic. The Merchant's forked beard could symbolize his duplicity, at which Chaucer only hints.

PHYSIOGNOMY

Physiognomy was a science that judged a person's temperament and character based on his or her anatomy. Physiognomy plays a significant role in Chaucer's descriptions of the pilgrims in the General Prologue. The most exaggerated facial features are those of the peasants. The Miller represents the stereotypical peasant physiognomy most clearly: round and ruddy, with a wart on his nose, the Miller appears rough and therefore suited to rough, simple work. The Pardoner's glaring eyes and limp hair illustrate his fraudulence.

Summary & Analysis

General Prologue: Introduction

Fragment I, lines 1–42

Summary

> *Whan that Aprill with his shoures soote*
> *The droghte of March hath perced to the roote . . .*
> *(See* QUOTATIONS, *p. 75)*

The narrator opens the General Prologue with a description of the return of spring. He describes the April rains, the burgeoning flowers and leaves, and the chirping birds. Around this time of year, the narrator says, people begin to feel the desire to go on a pilgrimage. Many devout English pilgrims set off to visit shrines in distant holy lands, but even more choose to travel to Canterbury to visit the relics of Saint Thomas Becket in Canterbury Cathedral, where they thank the martyr for having helped them when they were in need. The narrator tells us that as he prepared to go on such a pilgrimage, staying at a tavern in Southwark called the Tabard Inn, a great company of twenty-nine travelers entered. The travelers were a diverse group who, like the narrator, were on their way to Canterbury. They happily agreed to let him join them. That night, the group slept at the Tabard, and woke up early the next morning to set off on their journey. Before continuing the tale, the narrator declares his intent to list and describe each of the members of the group.

Analysis

The invocation of spring with which the General Prologue begins is lengthy and formal compared to the language of the rest of the Prologue. The first lines situate the story in a particular time and place, but the speaker does this in cosmic and cyclical terms, celebrating the vitality and richness of spring. This approach gives the opening lines a dreamy, timeless, unfocused quality, and it is therefore surprising when the narrator reveals that he's going to describe a pilgrimage that he himself took rather than telling a love story. A pilgrimage is a religious journey undertaken for penance and grace. As pilgrimages went, Canterbury was not a very difficult destination for an English person to reach. It was, therefore, very popular in fourteenth-century England, as the narrator mentions. Pilgrims traveled to visit the remains of Saint Thomas Becket, archbishop of Canterbury, who was murdered in 1170 by knights of King Henry II. Soon after his death, he became the most popular saint in England. The pilgrimage in *The Canterbury Tales* should not be thought of as an entirely solemn occasion, because it also offered the pilgrims an opportunity to abandon work and take a vacation.

In line 20, the narrator abandons his unfocused, all-knowing point of view, identifying himself as an actual person for the first time by inserting the first person—"I"—as he relates how he met the group of pilgrims while staying at the Tabard Inn. He emphasizes that this group, which he encountered by accident, was itself formed quite by chance (25–26). He then shifts into the first-person plural, referring to the pilgrims as "we" beginning in line 29, asserting his status as a member of the group.

The narrator ends the introductory portion of his prologue by noting that he has "tyme and space" to tell his narrative. His comments underscore the fact that he is writing some time after the events of his story, and that he is describing the characters from memory. He has spoken and met with these people, but he has waited a certain length of time before sitting down and describing them. His intention to describe each pilgrim as he or she *seemed* to him is also important, for it emphasizes that his descriptions are not only subject to his memory but are also shaped by his individual perceptions and opinions regarding each of the characters. He positions himself as a mediator between two groups: the group of pilgrims, of which he was a member, and us, the audience, whom the narrator explicitly addresses as "you" in lines 34 and 38.

On the other hand, the narrator's declaration that he will tell us about the "condicioun," "degree," and "array" (dress) of each of the pilgrims suggests that his portraits will be based on objective facts as well as his own opinions. He spends considerable time characterizing the group members according to their social positions. The pilgrims represent a diverse cross section of fourteenth-century English society. Medieval social theory divided society into three broad classes, called "estates": the military, the clergy, and the laity. (The nobility, not represented in the General Prologue, traditionally derives its title and privileges from military duties and service, so it is considered part of the military estate.) In the portraits that we will see in the rest of the General Prologue, the Knight and Squire represent the military estate. The clergy is represented by the Prioress (and her nun and three priests), the Monk, the Friar, and the Parson. The other characters, from the wealthy Franklin to the poor Plowman, are the members of the laity. These lay characters can be further subdivided into landowners (the Franklin), professionals (the Clerk, the Man of Law, the Guildsmen, the Physician, and the Shipman), laborers (the Cook and the Plowman), stewards (the Miller, the Manciple, and the Reeve), and church officers (the Summoner and the Pardoner). As we will see, Chaucer's descriptions of the various characters and their social roles reveal the influence of the medieval genre of estates satire.

GENERAL PROLOGUE: THE KNIGHT THROUGH THE MAN OF LAW

Fragment I, lines 43–330

SUMMARY

The narrator begins his character portraits with the Knight. In the narrator's eyes, the Knight is the noblest of the pilgrims, embodying military prowess, loyalty, honor, generosity, and good manners. The Knight conducts himself in a polite and mild fashion, never saying an unkind word about anyone. The Knight's son, who is about twenty years old, acts as his father's squire, or apprentice. Though the Squire has fought in battles with great strength and agility, like his father, he is also devoted to love. A strong, beautiful, curly-haired young man dressed in clothes embroidered with dainty flowers, the Squire fights in the hope of winning favor with his "lady." His talents are those of the courtly lover—singing, playing the flute, drawing, writing, and riding—and he loves so passionately that he gets little sleep at night. He is a dutiful son, and fulfills his responsibilities toward his father, such as carving his meat. Accompanying the Knight and Squire is the Knight's Yeoman, or freeborn servant. The Yeoman wears green from head to toe and carries an enormous bow and beautifully feathered arrows, as well as a sword and small shield. His gear and attire suggest that he is a forester.

Next, the narrator describes the Prioress, named Madame Eglentyne. Although the Prioress is not part of the royal court, she does her best to imitate its manners. She takes great care to eat her food daintily, to reach for food on the table delicately, and to wipe her lip clean of grease before drinking from her cup. She speaks French, but with a provincial English accent. She is compassionate toward animals, weeping when she sees a mouse caught in a trap, and feeding her dogs roasted meat and milk. The narrator says that her features are pretty, even her enormous forehead. On her arm she wears a set of prayer beads, from which hangs a gold brooch that features the Latin words for "Love Conquers All." Another nun and three priests accompany her.

The Monk is the next pilgrim the narrator describes. Extremely handsome, he loves hunting and keeps many horses. He is an outrider at his monastery (he looks after the monastery's business with the external world), and his horse's bridle can be heard jingling in the wind as clear and loud as a church bell. The Monk is aware that the rule of his monastic order discourages monks from engaging in activities like hunting, but he dismisses such strictures as worthless. The narrator says that he agrees with the Monk: why should the Monk drive himself crazy with study or manual labor? The fat, bald, and well-dressed Monk resembles a prosperous lord.

The next member of the company is the Friar—a member of a religious order who lives entirely by begging. This friar is jovial, pleasure-loving, well-spoken, and socially agreeable. He hears confessions, and assigns very easy penance to people who donate money. For this reason, he is very popular with wealthy landowners throughout the country. He justifies his leniency by arguing that donating money to friars is a sign of true repentance, even if the penitent is incapable of shedding tears. He also makes himself popular with innkeepers and barmaids, who can give him food and drink. He pays no attention to beggars and lepers because they can't help him or his fraternal order. Despite his vow of poverty, the donations he extracts allow him to dress richly and live quite merrily.

Tastefully attired in nice boots and an imported fur hat, the Merchant speaks constantly of his profits. The merchant is good at borrowing money, but clever enough to keep anyone from knowing that he is in debt. The narrator does not know his name. After the Merchant comes the Clerk, a thin and threadbare student of philosophy at Oxford, who devours books instead of food. The Man of Law, an influential lawyer, follows next. He is a wise character, capable of preparing flawless legal documents. The Man of Law is a very busy man, but he takes care to appear even busier than he actually is.

Analysis

The Canterbury Tales is more than an estates satire because the characters are fully individualized creations rather than simple good or bad examples of some ideal type. Many of them seem aware that they inhabit a socially defined role and seem to have made a conscious effort to redefine their prescribed role on their own terms. For instance, the Squire is training to occupy the same social role as his father, the Knight, but unlike his father he defines this role in terms of the ideals of courtly love rather than crusading. The Prioress is a nun, but she aspires to the manners and behavior of a lady of the court, and, like the Squire, incorporates the motifs of courtly love into her Christian vocation. Characters such as the Monk and the Friar, who more obviously corrupt or pervert their social roles, are able to offer a justification and a rationale for their behavior, demonstrating that they have carefully considered how to go about occupying their professions.

Within each portrait, the narrator praises the character being described in superlative terms, promoting him or her as an outstanding example of his or her type. At the same time, the narrator points out things about many of the characters that the reader would be likely to view as flawed or corrupt, to varying degrees. The narrator's naïve stance introduces many different ironies into the General Prologue. Though it is not always clear exactly how ironic the narrator is being, the reader can perceive a difference between what each character *should* be and what he or she is.

The narrator is also a character, and an incredibly complex one at that. Examination of the narrator's presentation of the pilgrims reveals some of his prejudices. The Monk's portrait, in which the narrator inserts his own judgment of the Monk into the actual portrait, is the clearest example of this. But most of the time, the narrator's opinions are more subtly present. What he does and doesn't discuss, the order in which he presents or recalls details, and the extent to which he records objective characteristics of the pilgrims are all crucial to our own ironic understanding of the narrator.

The Knight, the Squire, and the Yeoman

The Knight has fought in crusades the world over, and comes as close as any of the characters to embodying the ideals of his vocation. But even in his case, the narrator suggests a slight separation between the individual and the role: the Knight doesn't simply exemplify chivalry, truth, honor, freedom, and courtesy; he "loves" them.

His virtues are due to his self-conscious pursuit of clearly conceived ideals. Moreover, the Knight's comportment is significant. Not only is he a worthy warrior, he is prudent in the image of himself that he projects. His appearance is calculated to express humility rather than vainglory.

Whereas the narrator describes the Knight in terms of abstract ideals and battles, he describes the Knight's son, the Squire, mostly in terms of his aesthetic attractiveness. The Squire prepares to occupy the same role as his father, but he envisions that role differently, supplementing his father's devotion to military prowess and the Christian cause with the ideals of courtly love (see discussion of courtly love under "Themes, Motifs, and Symbols"). He displays all of the accomplishments and behaviors prescribed for the courtly lover: he grooms and dresses himself carefully, he plays and sings, he tries to win favor with his "lady," and he doesn't sleep at night because of his overwhelming love. It is important to recognize, however, that the Squire isn't simply in love because he is young and handsome; he has picked up all of his behaviors and poses from his culture.

The description of the Knight's servant, the Yeoman, is limited to an account of his physical appearance, leaving us with little upon which to base an inference about him as an individual. He is, however, quite well attired for someone of his station, possibly suggesting a self-conscious attempt to look the part of a forester.

The Prioress, the Monk, and the Friar

With the descriptions of the Prioress, the Monk, and the Friar, the level of irony with which each character is presented gradually increases. Like the Squire, the Prioress seems to have redefined her own role, imitating the behavior of a woman of the royal court and supplementing her religious garb with a courtly love motto: Love Conquers All. This does not necessarily imply that she is corrupt: Chaucer's satire of her is subtle rather than scathing. More than a personal culpability, the Prioress's devotion to courtly love demonstrates the universal appeal and influence of the courtly love tradition in Chaucer's time. Throughout *The Canterbury Tales*, Chaucer seems to question the popularity of courtly love in his own culture, and to highlight the contradictions between courtly love and Christianity.

The narrator focuses on the Prioress's table manners in minute detail, openly admiring her courtly manners. He seems mesmerized by her mouth, as he mentions her smiling, her singing, her French speaking, her eating, and her drinking. As if to apologize for dwelling so long on what he seems to see as her erotic manner, he moves to a consideration of her "conscience," but his decision to illustrate her great compassion by focusing on the way she treats her pets and reacts to a mouse is probably tongue-in-cheek. The Prioress emerges as a very realistically portrayed human being, but she seems somewhat lacking as a religious figure.

The narrator's admiring description of the Monk is more conspicuously satirical than that of the Prioress. The narrator zeroes in on the Monk with a vivid image: his bridle jingles as loud and clear as a chapel bell. This image is pointedly ironic, since the chapel is where the Monk should be but isn't. To a greater degree than the Squire or the Prioress, the Monk has departed from his prescribed role as defined by the founders of his order. He lives like a lord rather than a cleric. Hunting is an extremely expensive form of leisure, the pursuit of the upper classes. The narrator takes pains to point out that the Monk is aware of the rules of his order but scorns them.

Like the Monk, the Friar does not perform his function as it was originally conceived. Saint Francis, the prototype for begging friars, ministered specifically to beggars and lepers, the very people the Friar disdains. Moreover, the Friar doesn't just neglect his spiritual duties; he actually abuses them for his own profit. The description of his activities implies that he gives easy penance in order to get extra money, so that he can live well. Like the Monk, the Friar is ready with arguments justifying his reinterpretation of his role: beggars and lepers cannot help the Church, and giving money is a sure sign of penitence. The narrator strongly hints that the Friar is lecherous as well as greedy. The statement that he made many marriages at his own cost suggests that he found husbands for young women he had made pregnant. His white neck is a conventional sign of lecherousness.

THE MERCHANT, THE CLERK, AND THE MAN OF LAW

The Merchant, the Clerk, and the Man of Law represent three professional types. Though the narrator valiantly keeps up the pretense of praising everybody, the Merchant evidently taxes his ability to do so. The Merchant is in debt, apparently a regular occurrence, and his supposed cleverness at hiding his indebtedness is undermined by the fact that even the naïve narrator knows about it. Though the narrator would like to praise him, the Merchant hasn't even told the company his name.

Sandwiched between two characters who are clearly devoted to money, the threadbare Clerk appears strikingly oblivious to worldly concerns. However, the ultimate purpose of his study is unclear. The Man of Law contrasts sharply with the Clerk in that he has used his studies for monetary gain.

General Prologue: The Franklin through the Pardoner

Fragment I, lines 331–714

Summary

The white-bearded Franklin is a wealthy gentleman farmer, possessed of lands but not of noble birth. His chief attribute is his preoccupation with food, which is so plenteous in his house that his house seemed to snow meat and drink (344–345). The narrator next describes the five Guildsmen, all artisans. They are dressed in the livery, or uniform, of their guild. The narrator compliments their shiny dress and mentions that each was fit to be a city official. With them is their skillful Cook, whom Chaucer would praise fully were it not for the ulcer on his shin. The hardy Shipman wears a dagger on a cord around his neck. When he is on his ship, he steals wine from the merchant he is transporting while he sleeps.

The taffeta-clad Physician bases his practice of medicine and surgery on a thorough knowledge of astronomy and the four humors. He has a good setup with his apothecaries, because they make each other money. He is well acquainted with ancient and modern medical authorities, but reads little Scripture. He is somewhat frugal, and the narrator jokes that the doctor's favorite medicine is gold.

Next, the narrator describes the slightly deaf Wife of Bath. This keen seamstress is always first to the offering at Mass, and if someone goes ahead of her she gets upset. She wears head coverings to Mass that the narrator guesses must weigh ten pounds. She has had five husbands and has taken three pilgrimages to Jerusalem. She has also been to Rome, Cologne, and other exotic pilgrimage sites. Her teeth have gaps between them, and she sits comfortably astride her horse. The Wife is jolly and talkative, and she gives good love advice because she has had lots of experience.

A gentle and poor village Parson is described next. Pure of conscience and true to the teachings of Christ, the Parson enjoys preaching and instructing his parishioners, but he hates excommunicating those who cannot pay their tithes. He walks with his staff to visit all his parishioners, no matter how far away. He believes that a priest must be pure, because he serves as an example for his congregation, his flock. The Parson is dedicated to his parish and does not seek a better appointment. He is even kind to sinners, preferring to teach them by example rather than scorn. The parson is accompanied by his brother, a Plowman, who works hard, loves God and his neighbor, labors "for Christ's sake" (537), and pays his tithes on time.

The red-haired Miller loves crude, bawdy jokes and drinking. He is immensely stout and strong, able to lift doors off their hinges or knock them down by running at them with his head. He has a wart on his nose with bright red hairs sticking out of it like bristles, black nostrils, and a mouth like a furnace. He wears a sword and buckler, and loves to joke around and tell dirty stories. He steals from his customers, and plays the bagpipes.

The Manciple stocks an Inn of Court (school of law) with provisions. Uneducated though he is, this manciple is smarter than most of the lawyers he serves. The spindly, angry Reeve has hair so short that he reminds the narrator of a priest. He manages his lord's estate so well that he is able to hoard his own money and property in a miserly fashion. The Reeve is also a good carpenter, and he always rides behind everybody else.

The Summoner arraigns those accused of violating Church law. When drunk, he ostentatiously spouts the few Latin phrases he knows. His face is bright red from an unspecified disease. He uses his power corruptly for his own gain. He is extremely lecherous, and uses his position to dominate the young women in his jurisdiction. In exchange for a quart of wine, he would let another man sleep with his girlfriend for a year and then pardon the man completely.

The Pardoner, who had just been in the court of Rome, rides with the Summoner. He sings with his companion, and has long, flowing, yellow hair. The narrator mentions that the Pardoner thinks he rides very fashionably, with nothing covering his head. He has brought back many souvenirs from his trip to Rome. The narrator compares the Pardoner's high voice to that of a goat, and mentions that he thinks the Pardoner might have been a homosexual. The narrator mocks the Pardoner for his disrespectful manipulation of the poor for his own material gain. In charge of selling papal indulgences, he is despised by the Church and most churchgoers for counterfeiting pardons and pocketing the money. The Pardoner is a good preacher, storyteller, and singer, the narrator admits, although he argues it is only because he cheats people of their money in that way.

ANALYSIS
Again, the narrator describes many of the characters as though he had actually witnessed them doing things he has only heard them talk about. Other portraits, such as that of the Miller, are clearly shaped by class stereotypes.

THE FRANKLIN, THE GUILDSMEN, AND THE COOK
The Franklin and the five Guildsmen share with the Merchant and the Man of Law a devotion to material wealth, and the narrator praises them in terms of their possessions. The description of the Franklin's table is a lavish poetic tribute to hospitality and luxury. The Haberdasher, Carpenter, Weaver, Dyer, and Tapestry-Weaver are not individualized, and they don't tell their own tales. The narrator's approval of their pride in material displays of wealth is clearly satirical. The Cook, with his disgusting physical defect, is himself a display of the Guildsmen's material worth and prosperity.

THE SHIPMAN AND THE PHYSICIAN
The descriptions of the Shipman and the Physician are both barbed with keenly satiric turns of phrase implying dishonesty and avarice. The Shipman's theft of wine is slipped in among descriptions of his professional skills, and his brutality in battle is briefly noted in the midst of his other nautical achievements. The narrator gives an impressive catalog of the Physician's learning, but then interjects the startling comment that he neglects the Bible, implying that his care for the body comes at the expense of the soul. Moreover, the narrator's remarks about the Doctor's love of gold suggest that he is out to make money rather than to help others.

THE WIFE OF BATH
According to whether they infer Chaucer's implied attitude toward this fearless and outspoken woman as admiring or satirical, readers have interpreted the Wife of Bath as an expression either of Chaucer's proto-feminism or of his misogyny. Certainly, she embodies many of the traits that woman-hating writers of Chaucer's time attacked: she is vain, domineering, and lustful. But, at the same time, Chaucer portrays the Wife of Bath in such realistic and humane detail that it is hard to see her simply as a satire of an awful woman. Minor facets of her description, such as the gap between her teeth and her deafness, are expanded upon in the long prologue to her tale.

THE PARSON AND THE PLOWMAN

Coming after a catalog of very worldly characters, these two brothers stand out as rare examples of Christian ideals. The Plowman follows the Gospel, loving God and his neighbor, working for Christ's sake, and faithfully paying tithes to the Church. Their "worth" is thus of a completely different kind from that assigned to the valorous Knight or to the skilled and wealthy characters. The Parson has a more complicated role than the Plowman, and a more sophisticated awareness of his importance.

THE MILLER, THE MANCIPLE, AND THE REEVE

The Miller, the Manciple, and the Reeve are all stewards, in the sense that other people entrust them with their property. All three of them abuse that trust. Stewardship plays an important symbolic role in *The Canterbury Tales,* just as it does in the Gospels. In his parables, Jesus used stewardship as a metaphor for Christian life, since God calls the individual to account for his or her actions on the Day of Judgment, just as a steward must show whether he has made a profitable use of his master's property.

The Miller seems more demonic than Christian, with his violent and brutal habits, his mouth like a furnace, the angry red hairs sprouting from his wart, and his black nostrils. His "golden thumb" alludes to his practice of cheating his customers. The narrator ironically upholds the Manciple as a model of a good steward. The Manciple's employers are all lawyers, trained to help others to live within their means, but the Manciple is even shrewder than they are. The Reeve is depicted as a very skilled thief—one who can fool his own auditors, and who knows all the tricks of managers, servants, herdsmen, and millers because he is dishonest himself. Worst of all, he enjoys his master's thanks for lending his master the things he has stolen from him.

THE SUMMONER AND THE PARDONER

The Summoner and Pardoner, who travel together, are the most corrupt and debased of all the pilgrims. They are not members of holy orders but rather lay officers of the Church. Neither believes in what he does for the Church; instead, they both pervert their functions for their own gain and the corruption of others. The Summoner is a lecher and a drunk, always looking for a bribe. His diseased face suggests a diseased soul. The Pardoner is a more complicated figure. He sings beautifully in church and has a talent for beguiling his somewhat horrified audience. Longhaired and beardless, the

Pardoner's sexuality is ambiguous. The narrator remarks that he thought the Pardoner to be a gelding or a mare, possibly suggesting that he is either a eunuch or a homosexual. His homosexuality is further suggested by his harmonizing with the Summoner's "stif burdoun," which means the bass line of a melody but also hints at the male genitalia (673). The Pardoner will further disrupt the agreed-upon structure of the journey (friendly tale-telling) by launching into his indulgence-selling routine, turning his tale into a sermon he frequently uses to con people into feeding his greed. The narrator's disdain of the Pardoner may in part owe to his jealousy of the Pardoner's skill at mesmerizing an audience for financial gain—after all, this is a poet's goal as well.

General Prologue: Conclusion

Fragment I, lines 715–858

Summary

After introducing all of the pilgrims, the narrator apologizes for any possible offense the reader may take from his tales, explaining that he feels that he must be faithful in reproducing the characters' words, even if they are rude or disgusting. He cites Christ and Plato as support for his argument that it is best to speak plainly and tell the truth rather than to lie. He then returns to his story of the first night he spent with the group of pilgrims.

After serving the pilgrims a banquet and settling the bill with them, the Host of the tavern speaks to the group. He welcomes and compliments the company, telling them they are the merriest group of pilgrims to pass through his inn all year. He adds that he would like to contribute to their happiness, free of charge. He says that he is sure they will be telling stories as they travel, since it would be boring to travel in silence. Therefore, he proposes to invent some entertainment for them if they will unanimously agree to do as he says. He orders the group to vote, and the narrator comments that the group didn't think it would be worthwhile to argue or deliberate over the Host's proposition and agreed immediately.

The Host congratulates the group on its good decision. He lays out his plan: each of the pilgrims will tell two tales on the way to Canterbury and two more on the way back. Whomever the Host decides has told the most meaningful and comforting stories will receive a meal paid for by the rest of the pilgrims upon their return. The Host also declares that he will ride with the pilgrims and serve as their guide at his own cost. If anyone disputes his judgment, he says, that person must pay for the expenses of the pilgrimage.

The company agrees and makes the Host its governor, judge, and record keeper. They settle on a price for the supper prize and return to drinking wine. The next morning, the Host wakes everyone up and gathers the pilgrims together. After they have set off, he reminds the group of the agreement they made. He also reminds them that whoever disagrees with him must pay for everything spent along the way. He tells the group members to draw straws to decide who tells the first tale. The Knight wins and prepares to begin his tale.

ANALYSIS

The Host shows himself to be a shrewd businessman. Once he has taken the pilgrims' money for their dinners, he takes their minds away from what they have just spent by flattering them, complimenting them for their mirth. Equally quickly, he changes the focus of the pilgrimage. In the opening lines of the General Prologue, the narrator says that people go on pilgrimages to thank the martyr, who has helped them when they were in need (17–18). But Bailey (as the Host is later called) tells the group, "Ye goon to Caunterbury— God yow speede, / The blissful martir quite yow youre meede!" (769–770). He sees the pilgrimage as an economic transaction: the pilgrims travel to the martyr, and in return the martyr rewards them. The word "quite" means "repay," and it will become a major motif throughout the tales, as each character is put in a sort of debt by the previous character's tale, and must repay him or her with a new tale. Instead of traveling to reach a destination (the shrine of Saint Thomas Becket), the traveling becomes a contest, and the pilgrimage becomes about the journey itself rather than the destination. Bailey also stands to profit from the contest: the winner of the contest wins a free meal at his tavern, to be paid for by the rest of the contestants, all of whom will presumably eat with the winner and thus buy more meals from Bailey.

After creating the storytelling contest, Bailey quickly appoints himself its judge. Once the pilgrims have voted to participate in the contest, Bailey inserts himself as their ruler, and anyone who disagrees with him faces a strict financial penalty. Some have interpreted Bailey's speedy takeover of the pilgrimage as an allegory for the beginnings of absolute monarchy. The narrator refers to the Host as the group's "governour," "juge," and "reportour [record-keeper]"—all very legalistic terms (813–814).

THE KNIGHT'S TALE, PARTS I–II

From the beginning through Theseus's decision to hold the tournament Fragment I, lines 859–1880

SUMMARY: PART I

Long ago in Ancient Greece, a great conqueror and duke named Theseus ruled the city of Athens. One day, four women kneel in front of Theseus's horse and weep, halting his passage into the city. The eldest woman informs him that they are grieving the loss of their husbands, who were killed at the siege of the city of Thebes. Creon, the lord of Thebes, has dishonored them by refusing to bury or cremate their bodies. Enraged at the ladies' plight, Theseus marches on Thebes, which he easily conquers. After returning the bones of their husbands to the four women for the funeral rites, Theseus discovers two wounded enemy soldiers lying on the battle-field, nearing death. Rather than kill them, he mercifully heals the Theban soldiers' injuries, but condemns them to a life of imprisonment in an Athenian tower.

The prisoners, named Palamon and Arcite, are cousins and sworn brothers. Both live in the prison tower for several years. One spring morning, Palamon awakes early, looks out the window, and sees fair-haired Emelye, Theseus's sister-in-law. She is making flower garlands, "To doon honour to May" (1047). He falls in love and moans with heartache. His cry awakens Arcite, who comes to investigate the matter. As Arcite peers out the window, he too falls in love with the beautiful flower-clad maiden. They argue over her, but eventually realize the futility of such a struggle when neither can ever leave the prison.

One day, a duke named Perotheus, friend both to Theseus and Arcite, petitions for Arcite's freedom. Theseus agrees, on the condition that Arcite be banished permanently from Athens on pain of death. Arcite returns to Thebes, miserable and jealous of Palamon, who can still see Emelye every day from the tower. But Palamon, too, grows more sorrowful than ever; he believes that Arcite will lay siege to Athens and take Emelye by force. The knight poses the question to the listeners, rhetorically: who is worse off, Arcite or Palamon?

SUMMARY: PART II

Some time later, winged Mercury, messenger to the gods, appears to Arcite in a dream and urges him to return to Athens. By this time, Arcite has grown gaunt and frail from lovesickness. He realizes that he could enter the city disguised and not be recognized. He does so and takes on a job as a page in Emelye's chamber under the pseudonym Philostrate. This puts him close to Emelye but not close enough. Wandering in the woods one spring day, he fashions garlands of leaves and laments the conflict in his heart—his desire to return to Thebes and his need to be near his beloved. As it happens, Palamon has escaped from seven years of imprisonment that very day and hears Arcite's song and monologue while sneaking through the woods. They confront each other, each claiming the right to Emelye. Arcite challenges his old friend to a duel the next day. They meet in a field and bludgeon each other ruthlessly.

Theseus, out on a hunt, finds these two warriors brutally hacking away at each other. Palamon reveals their identities and love for Emelye. He implores the duke to justly decide their fate, suggesting that they both deserve to die. Theseus is about to respond by killing them, but the women of his court—especially his queen and Emelye—intervene, pleading for Palamon and Arcite's lives. The duke consents and decides instead to hold a tournament fifty weeks from that day. The two men will be pitted against one another, each with a hundred of the finest men he can gather. The winner will be awarded Emelye's hand.

Analysis

The Knight's Tale is a romance that encapsulates the themes, motifs, and ideals of courtly love: love is like an illness that can change the lover's physical appearance, the lover risks death to win favor with his lady, and he is inspired to utter eloquent poetic complaints. The lovers go without sleep because they are tormented by their love, and for many years they pine away hopelessly for an unattainable woman. The tale is set in mythological Greece, but Chaucer's primary source for it is Boccaccio's Teseida, an Italian poem written about thirty years before The Canterbury Tales. As was typical of medieval and Renaissance romances, ancient Greece is imagined as quite similar to feudal Europe, with knights and dukes instead of heroes, and various other medieval features.

Some critics have suggested that the Knight's Tale is an allegory, in which each character represents an abstract idea or theme. For example, Arcite and Palamon might represent the active and the contemplative life, respectively. But it is difficult to convincingly interpret the tale based on a distinction between the two lovers, or to find a moral based on their different actions. Palamon and Arcite are quite similar, and neither one seems to have the stronger claim on Emelye.

The main theme of the tale is the instability of human life—joy and suffering are never far apart from one another, and nobody is safe from disaster. Moreover, when one person's fortunes are up, another person's are down. This theme is expressed by the pattern of the narrative, in which descriptions of good fortune are quickly followed by disasters, and characters are subject to dramatic reversals of fortune. When the supplicating widows interrupt Theseus's victory procession home to Athens, he senses that their grief is somehow connected to his joy and asks them if they grieve out of envy. But one of the widows formulates the connection differently, pointing out that they are on opposite sides of Fortune's "false wheel" (925).

Soon, the widows' husbands' remains are returned to them, and Theseus once again emerges victorious. But as soon as the widows are raised up by Fortune's wheel, Palamon and Arcite are discovered cast down, close to death, and Theseus imprisons them for life. But, no sooner are Palamon's and Arcite's fortunes dashed down than Emelye appears in the garden outside their prison as a symbol of spring and renewed life. When Arcite wins his freedom, each of the friends thinks that his condition is worse than the other's.

Good fortune and bad fortune seem connected to one another in a pattern, suggesting that some kind of cosmic or moral order underlies the apparently random mishaps and disasters of the narrative. There are other such repeated elements in the story. The widows who supplicate for their husbands' remains at the story's opening are mirrored by Emelye and Theseus's queen, who supplicate Theseus to spare Palamon and Arcite's lives. Palamon's appeal to Theseus to rightly judge their quarrel echoes the knight's appeal to the listeners to decide who is more miserable. Additionally, when Arcite wanders in the woods, singing and fashioning garlands, he echoes Palamon's first vision of Emelye through the tower window, when he saw her making garlands. Both acts take place in the month of May.

The Knight's Tale, Parts III–IV

Theseus's construction of the stadium through the end of the tale Fragment I, lines 1881–3108

Summary: Part III

Theseus prepares for the tournament by constructing an enormous stadium. By its gate, he erects three temples to the gods—one for Venus, the goddess of love; one for Mars, the god of war; and one for Diana, the goddess of chastity. The Knight provides a lengthy description of each temple. The tournament nears, spectators assemble, and both Palamon and Arcite arrive with impressive armies. The Sunday before the tournament, Palamon visits the temple of Venus and supplicates her in the night. He tells her of his desire for Emelye and requests that she bring him victory in the name of love. The statue of Venus makes an enigmatic "sign" (the reader isn't told what the sign is), which Palamon interprets as a positive answer, and he departs confident. That dawn, Emelye also rises and goes to the temple of Diana. Desirous to remain a virgin—"a mayden al my lyf" (2305)—she begs Diana to prevent the impending marriage. But an image of Diana appears and informs her that she must marry one of the Thebans. Obedient, Emelye retires to her chamber.

Arcite walks to the temple of Mars and begs the god of war for victory in the battle. He, too, receives a positive sign: the doors of the temple clang, and he hears the statue of Mars whisper, "Victorie!" (2433). Like Palamon, Arcite departs the temple in high hopes for the coming day. The scene then shifts to the gods themselves. Saturn, Venus's father, assures her cryptically that despite Mars's aid to Arcite, Palamon will have his lady in the end.

Summary: Part IV

> *The Firste Moevere of the cause above,*
> *Whan he first made the faire cheyne of love,*
> *Greet was th'effect, and heigh was his entente.*
> (See QUOTATIONS, p. 75)

After much feasting, the spectators assemble in the stadium. The magnificent armies enter, appearing evenly matched. After Theseus has sternly delivered the rules, the bloody battle of flashing swords and maces begins. Though Palamon fights valiantly, Arcite sees his chance and brings Palamon "to the stake"—he claims him with a sword at his throat. Emelye rejoices as Theseus proclaims Arcite victorious.

Venus, on the other hand, weeps with shame that her knight lost, until Saturn calms her and signals that all is not over. At Saturn's request, the earth shakes beneath Arcite as he rides toward Theseus. The knight's horse throws him, crushing his chest. Gravely wounded, the company transports Arcite to bed, where physicians attempt in vain to heal him. Arcite expresses his love to Emelye, and then tells her that if she decides to marry another, she should remember Palamon, who possesses the qualities of a worthy knight—"trouthe, honour, knyghthede, / Wysdom, humblesse" (2789–2790).

All of Athens mourns Arcite's death. Emelye, Theseus, and Palamon are inconsolable. Theseus's father, Egeus, takes Theseus aside and tells him that every man must live and die—life is a journey through woe that must, at some point, come to an end. After some years pass, the mourners heal, with the exception of Emelye and Palamon, who continue to go about sorrowfully, dressed in black. During one parliament at Athens, Theseus berates the two for grieving too much. He reminds them that God ordains that all must die, and refusal to accept death is therefore folly. He requests that they cease mourning, and that his wife's sister take Palamon for her husband and lord. They obey, and as they realize the wisdom of Theseus's advice over many years, Emelye and Palamon enjoy a long, loving, and happy marriage.

ANALYSIS

Because Egeus has lived long enough to witness Fortune's rising and falling pattern, he is the only human character in the Knight's Tale who understands that Fortune's wheel is the plot's driving force. Egeus is therefore the only man capable of comforting Theseus amid the general lament over Arcite's accidental death. In his final speech to Palamon and Emelye, Theseus shows that he has learned his lesson from Egeus. Echoing the old man's words, the duke argues that excessive mourning over disaster is inappropriate. His speech conveys a message of humility, instead of an attempt to explain the meaning of Arcite's death. A benevolent order may exist in the universe, Theseus asserts, but human beings should not seek to pry into it, or set themselves against it by prolonging mourning too long.

The gods, whose role is to develop instability in the lives of the characters, are the instruments of Fortune. The Knight's extensive descriptions of the symbolic decorations of the temples of Venus, Mars, and Diana help shed light on the gods' roles. The walls in Venus's temple depict the traditional sufferings of the courtly lover—

sleeplessness, sighing, and burning desire. But they also portray the sinfulness that love can cause—lust, jealousy, idleness, and adultery—a more Christian, moralistic message. Moreover, these walls also present love's invincibility and irresistibility, in scenes taken from Ovid's *Metamorphoses*. The relationship among these three ideas of love is left unresolved.

Mars's temple is also remarkable. Instead of representing the glories of war or battle with which the Knight is well acquainted, the walls display hypocrites, traitors, and murderers, together with disasters that have nothing to do with war, such as the cook who is scalded despite his use of a long ladle. Diana's portrayal is the most ambivalent of the three. Traditionally, she is the goddess of chastity and protector of virgins, but everything depicted on her temple's walls suggests that she causes change. Many of the images are of friends or enemies that she transformed, as told in Ovid's *Metamorphoses*. Diana herself is symbolically represented by a moon that is waxing but that will soon begin to wane. The imagery in her temple, and her refusal to grant Emelye her prayer that she remain a virgin, indicate that there is no refuge, even in chastity, from the transformations human beings must undergo in life.

The decoration of each of the three temples, then, shows the wills of the gods as opposite to human desires. Venus and Mars are both represented as forces that cause catastrophe and suffering, rather than glory and happiness, in human life. Whereas Venus represents emotional and spiritual sources of suffering, Mars represents all of the violent and brutal physical perils that await humans, whether through accident or malice. And Diana is represented as a force who will not allow things to stay the same.

Saturn is not depicted, but his decision about how to reconcile the conflict between Mars and Venus reveals his understanding of his role, as does his description of himself, which strongly echoes the description of Mars's temple. Saturn associates himself with drowning, strangling, imprisonment, secret poisoning, and other forms of vengeance. The major difference between Mars and Saturn is that Saturn claims that his journey through the zodiac is much longer than that of the others, and that his actions are part of an overall plan that emerges over a long period of time. Saturn's disasters represent a kind of correction, or balancing of the scales, ensuring that everything is overturned and transformed by the passage of time.

Yet, there is some suggestion in the Knight's Tale that humans can affect their own destinies. Several major shifts in the plot come about when one character intercedes on another's behalf. The weeping women in the opening intercede on behalf of their dead husbands, and Theseus conquers Thebes. Perotheus intercedes on Arcite's behalf, and Arcite is let out of prison. The court women interrupt to plead that Theseus spare the two soldiers' lives.

Some critics have suggested that in this pattern of intercession Chaucer presents us with an ideal form of government: no man can govern entirely on his own. Truly good government is accomplished with the help of an outside party that stops the ruler from behaving tyrannically. Twice, women prevent Theseus from acting entirely on his own, a good friend is able to intervene to rescue Arcite, and Arcite himself influences Theseus's desire to see Emelye and Palamon married. Some critics further interpret this need for counsel along gender lines. It is no accident, they suggest, that *women* stop Theseus from ignoring the burial rites of their husbands, and from killing Palamon and Arcite. These critics believe that this female intercession means that every good male governor needs and depends upon wifely counsel to keep him from becoming ruthless.

THE MILLER'S PROLOGUE AND TALE

Fragment I, lines 3109–3854

SUMMARY

The pilgrims applaud the Knight's Tale, and the pleased Host asks the Monk to match it. Before the Monk can utter a word, however, the Miller interrupts. Drunk and belligerent, he promises that he has a "noble" tale that will repay the Knight's (3126). The Host tries to persuade the Miller to let some "bettre" man tell the next tale (3130). When the Miller threatens to leave, however, the Host acquiesces. After the Miller reminds everyone that he is drunk and therefore shouldn't be held accountable for anything he says, he introduces his tale as a legend and a life of a carpenter and of his wife, and of how a clerk made a fool of the carpenter, which everyone understands to mean that the clerk slept with the carpenter's wife (3141–3143). The Reeve shouts out his immediate objection to such ridicule, but the Miller insists on proceeding with his tale. He points out that he is married himself, but doesn't worry whether some other man is sleeping with his wife, because it is none of his business. The narrator apologizes to us in advance for the tale's bawdiness, and warns that those who are easily offended should skip to another tale.

The Miller begins his story: there was once an Oxford student named Nicholas, who studied astrology and was well acquainted with the art of love. Nicholas boarded with a wealthy but ignorant old carpenter named John, who was jealous and highly possessive of his sexy eighteen-year-old wife, Alisoun. One day, the carpenter leaves, and Nicholas and Alisoun begin flirting. Nicholas grabs Alisoun, and she threatens to cry for help. He then begins to cry, and after a few sweet words, she agrees to sleep with him when it is safe to do so. She is worried that John will find out, but Nicholas is confident he can outwit the carpenter.

Nicholas is not alone in desiring Alisoun. A merry, vain parish clerk named Absolon also fancies Alisoun. He serenades her every night, buys her gifts, and gives her money, but to no avail—Alisoun loves Nicholas. Nicholas devises a plan that will allow him and Alisoun to spend an entire night together. He has Alisoun tell John that Nicholas is ill. John sends a servant to check on his boarder, who arrives to find Nicholas immobile, staring at the ceiling. When the servant reports back to John, John is not surprised, saying that madness is what one gets for inquiring into "Goddes pryvetee," which is what he believes Nicholas's astronomy studies amount to. Nevertheless, he feels sorry for the student and goes to check on him.

Nicholas tells John he has had a vision from God and offers to tell John about it. He explains that he has foreseen a terrible event. The next Monday, waters twice as great as Noah's flood will cover the land, exterminating all life. The carpenter believes him and fears for his wife, just what Nicholas had hoped would occur. Nicholas instructs John to fasten three tubs, each loaded with provisions and an ax, to the roof of the barn. On Monday night, they will sleep in the tubs, so that when the flood comes, they can release the tubs, hack through the roof, and float until the water subsides. Nicholas also warns John that it is God's commandment that they may do nothing but pray once they are in the tubs—no one is to speak a word.

Monday night arrives, and Nicholas, John, and Alisoun ascend by ladder into the hanging tubs. As soon as the carpenter begins to snore, Nicholas and Alisoun climb down, run back to the house, and sleep together in the carpenter's bed. In the early dawn, Absolon passes by. Hoping to stop in for a kiss, or perhaps more, from Alisoun, Absalon sidles up to the window and calls to her. She harshly replies that she loves another. Absolon persists, and Alisoun offers him one quick kiss in the dark.

Absolon leaps forward eagerly, offering a lingering kiss. But it is not her lips he finds at the window, but her "naked ers [arse]" (3734). She and Nicholas collapse with laughter, while Absolon blindly tries to wipe his mouth. Determined to avenge Alisoun's prank, Absolon hurries back into town to the blacksmith and obtains a red-hot iron poker. He returns with it to the window and knocks again, asking for a kiss and promising Alisoun a golden ring. This time, Nicholas, having gotten up to relieve himself anyway, sticks his rear out the window and farts thunderously in Absolon's face. Absolon brands Nicholas's buttocks with the poker. Nicholas leaps up and cries out, "Help! Water! Water!" (3815). John, still hanging from the roof, wakes up and assumes Nicholas's cries mean that the flood has come. He grabs the ax, cuts free the tub, and comes crashing to the ground, breaking his arm. The noise and commotion attract many of the townspeople. The carpenter tells the story of the predicted flood, but Nicholas and Alisoun pretend ignorance, telling everyone that the carpenter is mad. The townspeople laugh that all have received their dues, and the Miller merrily asks that God save the company.

ANALYSIS

> *Thus swyved was this carpenteris wyf,*
> *For al his kepyng and his jalousye;*
> *And Absolon hath kist hir nether ye;*
> *And Nicholas is scalded in the towte.*
>
> *(See* QUOTATIONS, *p. 77)*

In the Miller's Prologue, we perceive tension between social classes for the first time in *The Canterbury Tales*. The Host clearly wants the Monk to tell the second tale, so that the storytelling proceeds according to social rank. By butting in, the Miller upsets the Host's plan. Like the Knight's Tale, which fits his honorable and virtuous personality, the Miller's Tale is stereotypical of the Miller's bawdy character and low station. However, nothing about the drunken, immoral, and brutal Miller could possibly prepare the reader for the Miller's elegant verse and beautiful imagery. The Miller's description of Alisoun draws on a completely different stock of images from the Knight's depiction of Emelye, but it is no less effective. Whereas Emelye is compared to a rose, a lily, the spring, and an angel, Alisoun's body is delicate and slender like a weasel, her apron is as white as morning milk, and her features are compared to plums and pear trees. The Miller's imagery is less conventional and less elevated than the Knight's, drawn instead from the details of village or farm life.

Although the narrator is unforgiving in his depiction of the drunk, rowdy Miller, whom he presents according to the stereotypes of the Miller's class and profession, there are a few intriguing points of similarity between the narrator and the Miller. For instance, the Miller apologizes for the tale he is about to tell, and transfers all blame to the "ale of Southwerk"—in effect, to the Host himself (3140). Thirty lines later, the narrator himself makes a similar apology, and reminds his audience to blame the Miller if it finds the tale offensive. Also, the Miller begins his story by giving little portraits of each of his characters, just as the narrator begins his story of the pilgrimage by outlining each of its members.

The Host asks the Monk to "quite," or repay, the Knight's Tale (3119). But when the Miller interrupts and cries out that he can "quite the Knyghtes [Knight's] tale," he changes the word somewhat to mean "revenge" (3127). Indeed, the Miller does take "revenge" upon the Knight to an extent. Just as he transforms the meaning of the word "quite," the Miller takes several of the themes from the Knight's Tale and alters them. For instance, the Knight's Tale suggested that human suffering is part of a divine plan that mortals cannot hope to know. In a completely different tone and context, the Miller, too, cautions against prying into "God's pryvetee," meaning God's secrets (3164). He first raises this idea in his Prologue, arguing that a man shouldn't take it upon himself to assume that his wife is unfaithful. In the Miller's Tale, John repeats the caution against prying into "God's pryvetee." Several times, John scolds Nicholas for trying to know "God's pryvetee," but when Nicholas actually offers to let John in on his secret, John jumps at the chance. John also jealously tries to control his young wife, reminding us that the Miller equated an attempt to know God's "pryvetee" with a husband's attempt to know about his wife's "private parts." The two round tubs that the foolish carpenter hangs from the roof of his barn, one on either side of a long trough, suggest an obscene visual pun on this vulgar meaning of "God's pryvetee."

The Miller's Tale also responds to the Knight's by turning the Knight's courtly love into a burlesque farce. The Miller places his lovers' intrigues in a lower-class context, satirizing the pretensions of long-suffering courtly lovers by portraying Nicholas and Alisoun in a frank and sexually graphic manner—Nicholas seduces Alisoun by grabbing her by the pudendum, or "queynte" (3276). Absolon, the parish clerk, represents a parody of the conventional courtly lover. He stays awake at night, patiently woos his lady by means of go-betweens, sings and plays guitar, and aspires to be Alisoun's page or servant. For his pains, all he gets is the chance to kiss Alisoun's anus and to be farted on by Nicholas.

In addition to parodying tales of courtly love, the Miller's Tale also plays with the medieval genres of fabliaux and of mystery plays. Fabliaux are bawdy, comic tales that build to a ridiculous and complex climax usually hinging on some joke or trick. Nicholas is parody of the traditional clever cleric in a fabliau. As the deviser of the scheme to trick John, he seems to be attempting to write his own fabliau, although Absolon foils his plan. Yet, John is still the big loser in the end. The moral of the play is that John should not have married someone so young: "Men sholde wedden after hire estaat [their estate], / For youthe and elde [old age] is often at debaat" (3229–3230). Justice is served in the Miller's eyes when Alisoun commits adultery, because she revenges her husband "[f]or . . . his jalousye" (3851). Despite their differences, the two clerics ally at the story's end to dupe the carpenter, and so nobody believes John's story about Nicholas's trick.

The Miller's Tale also includes references to different scenes acted out in medieval mystery plays. Mystery plays, which typically enacted stories of God, Jesus, and the saints, were the main source of biblical education for lay folk in the Middle Ages. As John's gullibility shows, his education through mystery plays means that he has only a slight understanding of the Bible. The Miller begins his biblical puns in his Prologue, when he says that he will speak in "[Pontius] Pilates" place. His statement that he will tell "a legende and a lyf / Bothe of a carpenter and of his wyf" is a reference to the story of Joseph and Mary. "Legends and lives" were written and told of the saints, and the story in which Joseph finds out that Mary is pregnant (and the many jokes that could be made about Mary being unfaithful) was a common subject of mystery plays. The stories of Noah's flood, and of Noah's wife, are also obviously twisted around by the Miller. These biblical puns work up to the climax of the tale. When he says that Nicholas's fart was as great as a "thonder-dent," the Miller aligns Nicholas—the creator of the action—with God (3807). Absolon, who cries out, "My soule bitake I unto Sathanas [Satan]" (3750), becomes a version of the devil, who damns God by sticking him with his red-hot poker. The result of Absolon's actions is that John falls from the roof in a pun on the fall of humanity.

THE WIFE OF BATH'S PROLOGUE

*From the beginning through the Wife of Bath's description of
her first three husbands Fragment III, lines 1–451*

SUMMARY

The Wife of Bath begins the Prologue to her tale by establishing
herself as an authority on marriage, due to her extensive personal
experience with the institution. Since her first marriage at the tender
age of twelve, she has had five husbands. She says that many people
have criticized her for her numerous marriages, most of them on the
basis that Christ went only once to a wedding, at Cana in Galilee.
The Wife of Bath has her own views of Scripture and God's plan.
She says that men can only guess and interpret what Jesus meant
when he told a Samaritan woman that her fifth husband was not
her husband. With or without this bit of Scripture, no man has ever
been able to give her an exact reply when she asks to know how
many husbands a woman may have in her lifetime. God bade us
to wax fruitful and multiply, she says, and that is the text that she
wholeheartedly endorses. After all, great Old Testament figures, like
Abraham, Jacob, and Solomon, enjoyed multiple wives at once. She
admits that many great Fathers of the Church have proclaimed the
importance of virginity, such as the Apostle Paul. But, she reasons,
even if virginity is important, someone must be procreating so that
virgins can be created. Leave virginity to the perfect, she says, and
let the rest of us use our gifts as best we may—and her gift, doubt-
less, is her sexual power. She uses this power as an "instrument" to
control her husbands.

At this point, the Pardoner interrupts. He is planning to marry
soon and worries that his wife will control his body, as the Wife of
Bath describes. The Wife of Bath tells him to have patience and to
listen to the whole tale to see if it reveals the truth about marriage.
Of her five husbands, three have been "good" and two have been
"bad." The first three were good, she admits, mostly because they
were rich, old, and submissive. She laughs to recall the torments
that she put these men through and recounts a typical conversation
that she had with her older husbands. She would accuse her husband of having an affair, launching into a tirade in which she would
charge him with a bewildering array of accusations. If one of her
husbands got drunk, she would claim he said that every wife is out
to destroy her husband. He would then feel guilty and give her what

she wanted. All of this, the Wife of Bath tells the rest of the pilgrims, was a pack of lies—her husbands never held these opinions, but she made these claims to give them grief. Worse, she would tease her husbands in bed, refusing to give them full satisfaction until they promised her money. She admits proudly to using her verbal and sexual power to bring her husbands to total submission.

ANALYSIS

In her lengthy Prologue, the Wife of Bath recites her autobiography, announcing in her very first word that "experience" will be her guide. Yet, despite her claim that experience is her sole authority, the Wife of Bath apparently feels the need to establish her authority in a more scholarly way. She imitates the ways of churchmen and scholars by backing up her claims with quotations from Scripture and works of antiquity. The Wife carelessly flings around references as textual evidence to buttress her argument, most of which don't really correspond to her points. Her reference to Ptolemy's *Almageste,* for instance, is completely erroneous—the phrase she attributes to that book appears nowhere in the work. Although her many errors display her lack of real scholarship, they also convey Chaucer's mockery of the churchmen present, who often misused Scripture to justify their devious actions.

The text of the Wife of Bath's Prologue is based in the medieval genre of allegorical "confession." In a morality play, a personified vice such as Gluttony or Lust "confesses" his or her sins to the audience in a life story. The Wife is exactly what the medieval Church saw as a "wicked woman," and she is proud of it—from the very beginning, her speech has undertones of conflict with her patriarchal society. Because the statements that the Wife of Bath attributes to her husbands were taken from a number of satires published in Chaucer's time, which half-comically portrayed women as unfaithful, superficial, evil creatures, always out to undermine their husbands, feminist critics have often tried to portray the Wife as one of the first feminist characters in literature.

This interpretation is weakened by the fact that the Wife of Bath herself conforms to a number of these misogynist and misogamist (antimarriage) stereotypes. For example, she describes herself as sexually voracious but at the same time as someone who only has sex to get money, thereby combining two contradictory stereotypes. She also describes how she dominated her husband, playing on a fear that was common to men, as the Pardoner's nervous interjection reveals. Despite their contradictions, all of these ideas about women were used by men to support a hierarchy in which men dominated women.

THE WIFE OF BATH'S PROLOGUE (CONTINUED)

From the Wife of Bath's description of her fourth husband through the end of her prologue Fragment III, lines 452–856

SUMMARY

The Wife of Bath begins her description of her two "bad" husbands. Her fourth husband, whom she married when still young, was a reveler, and he had a "paramour," or mistress (454). Remembering her wild youth, she becomes wistful as she describes the dancing and singing in which she and her fourth husband used to indulge. Her nostalgia reminds her of how old she has become, but she says that she pays her loss of beauty no mind. She will try to be merry, for, though she has lost her "flour," she will try to sell the "bran" that remains. Realizing that she has digressed, she returns to the story of her fourth husband. She confesses that she was his purgatory on Earth, always trying to make him jealous. He died while she was on a pilgrimage to Jerusalem.

Of her fifth husband, she has much more to say. She loved him, even though he treated her horribly and beat her. He was coy and flattering in bed, and always won her back. Women, the Wife says, always desire what is forbidden them, and run away from whatever pursues or is forced upon them. This husband was also different from the other four because she married him for love, not money. He was a poor ex-student who boarded with the Wife's friend and confidante.

When she first met this fifth husband, Jankyn, she was still married to her fourth. While walking with him one day, she told him that she would marry him if she were widowed. She lied to him and told him he had enchanted her, and that she had dreamed that he would kill her as she slept, filling her bed with blood, which signifies gold. But, she confides to her listeners, all of this was false: she never had such a dream. She loses her place in the story momentarily, then resumes with her fourth husband's funeral. She made a big show of crying, although, she admits, she actually cried very little since she already had a new husband lined up.

As she watched Jankyn carry her husband's casket, she fell in love with him. He was only twenty and she forty, but she was always a lusty woman and thought she could handle his youth. But, she says, she came to regret the age difference, because he would not suffer her abuse like her past husbands and gave some of his own abuse in return. He had a "book of wicked wives" she recalls, called *Valerie and Theofraste*. This book contained the stories of the most deceitful wives in history. It began with Eve, who brought all mankind into sin by first taking the apple in the Garden of Eden; from there, it chronicled Delilah's betrayal of Samson, Clytemnestra's murder of Agamemnon, and other famous stories. Jankyn would torment the Wife of Bath (whom we learn in line 804 is named Alisoun) by reading out of this book at night.

One evening, out of frustration, the Wife tears three pages out of the book and punches Jankyn in the face. Jankyn repays her by striking her on the head, which is the reason, she explains in line 636, that she is now deaf in one ear. She cries out that she wants to kiss him before she dies, but when he comes over, she hits him again. They finally manage a truce, in which he hands over all of his meager estate to her, and she acts kindly and loving.

Her tale of her marriages finished, the Wife announces that she will tell her story, eliciting laughter from the Friar, who exclaims, "This is a long preamble of a tale!" (831). The Summoner tells him to shut up, and they exchange some angry words. The Host quiets everybody down and allows the Wife of Bath to begin her story.

ANALYSIS

In her discussion of her fourth and fifth husbands, the Wife of Bath begins to let her true feelings show through her argumentative rhetoric. Her language becomes even less controlled, and she loses her place several times (at line 585, for instance), as she begins to react to her own story, allowing her words to affect her own train of thought. Her sensitivity about her age begins to show through, and, as she reveals psychological depth, she becomes a more realistic, sympathetic, and compelling character.

When the Wife of Bath describes how she fell in love with her fifth husband, despite her pragmatism, she reveals her softer side. She recognizes that he used the same tactics against her as she used against other men, but she cannot stop herself from desiring him. Jankyn even uses one of the satires against women to aggravate her, the kind of satire that the Wife mocked earlier in her Prologue.

Despite all this, we can see that Jankyn, though the most aggravating of her husbands, is the only one that she admits she truly loved. Even as she brags about her shameless manipulation of her husbands and claims that her sexual powers can conquer anyone, she retains a deep fondness for the one man she could not control.

The Wife seems to enjoy the act of arguing more than the end of deriving an answer by logic. To explain why clerks (meaning church writers) treat wives so badly, for example, she employs three different arguments. First, she blames the entire religious establishment, claiming that church writings breed hostility toward wives because they were written by men (690–696). Then, she gives an astrological explanation, asserting that the children of Mercury (scholars) and of Venus (lovers) always contradict one another. A third reason she gives is that when clerks grow old, their impotence and decreased virility makes them hostile and slanderous toward wives (705–710).

Twice in her Prologue, the Wife calls attention to her habit of lying—"and al was fals," she states (382, 582). These statements certainly highlight our awareness of the fact that she's giving a performance, and they also put her entire life story in question. We are left wondering to what extent we should even believe the "experience" of the Wife of Bath, and whether she is not, in fact, a mean-spirited satire on Chaucer's part, meant to represent the fickleness of women.

The Wife of Bath's Tale

Fragment III, lines 857–1264

Summary

In the days of King Arthur, the Wife of Bath begins, the isle of Britain was full of fairies and elves. Now, those creatures are gone because their spots have been taken by the friars and other mendicants that seem to fill every nook and cranny of the isle. And though the friars rape women, just as the incubi did in the days of the fairies, the friars only cause women dishonor—the incubi always got them pregnant.

In Arthur's court, however, a young, lusty knight comes across a beautiful young maiden one day. Overcome by lust and his sense of his own power, he rapes her. The court is scandalized by the crime and decrees that the knight should be put to death by decapitation. However, Arthur's queen and other ladies of the court intercede on his behalf and ask the king to give him one chance to save his own life. Arthur, wisely obedient to wifely counsel, grants their request. The queen presents the knight with the following challenge: if, within one year, he can discover what women want most in the world and report his findings back to the court, he will keep his life. If he cannot find the answer to the queen's question, or if his answer is wrong, he will lose his head.

The knight sets forth in sorrow. He roams throughout the country, posing the question to every woman he meets. To the knight's dismay, nearly every one of them answers differently. Some claim that women love money best, some honor, some jolliness, some looks, some sex, some remarriage, some flattery, and some say that women most want to be free to do as they wish. Finally, says the Wife, some say that women most want to be considered discreet and secretive, although she argues that such an answer is clearly untrue, since no woman can keep a secret. As proof, she retells Ovid's story of Midas. Midas had two ass's ears growing under his hair, which he concealed from everybody except his wife, whom he begged not to disclose his secret. She swore she would not, but the secret burned so much inside her that she ran down to a marsh and whispered her husband's secret to the water. The Wife then says that if her listeners would like to hear how the tale ends, they should read Ovid.

She returns to her story of the knight. When his day of judgment draws near, the knight sorrowfully heads for home. As he rides near a forest, he sees a large group of women dancing and decides to approach them to ask his question. But as he approaches, the group vanishes, and all he can see is an ugly old woman. The woman asks if she can be of help, and the knight explains his predicament and promises to reward her if she can help him. The woman tells the knight that he must pledge himself to her in return for her help, and the knight, having no options left, gladly consents. She then guarantees that his life will be saved.

The knight and the old woman travel together to the court, where, in front of a large audience, the knight tells the queen the answer with which the old woman supplied him: what women most desire is to be in charge of their husbands and lovers. The women agree resoundingly that this is the answer, and the queen spares the knight's life. The old hag comes forth and publicly asks the knight to marry her. The knight cries out in horror. He begs her to take his material possessions rather than his body, but she refuses to yield, and in the end he is forced to consent. The two are married in a small, private wedding and go to bed together the same night. Throughout the entire ordeal, the knight remains miserable.

While in bed, the loathsome hag asks the knight why he is so sad. He replies that he could hardly bear the shame of having such an ugly, lowborn wife. She does not take offense at the insult, but calmly asks him whether real "gentillesse," or noble character, can be hereditary (1109). There have been sons of noble fathers, she argues, who were shameful and villainous, though they shared the same blood. Her family may be poor, but real poverty lies in covetousness, and real riches lie in having little and wanting nothing. She offers the knight a choice: either he can have her be ugly but loyal and good, or he can have her young and fair but also coquettish and unfaithful. The knight ponders in silence. Finally, he replies that he would rather trust her judgment, and he asks her to choose whatever she thinks best. Because the knight's answer gave the woman what she most desired, the authority to choose for herself, she becomes both beautiful *and* good. The two have a long, happy marriage, and the woman becomes completely obedient to her husband. The Wife of Bath concludes with a plea that Jesus Christ send all women husbands who are young, meek, and fresh in bed, and the grace to outlive their husbands.

Analysis

> *"Wommen desiren to have sovereyntee*
> *As wel over hir housbond as hir love,*
> *And for to been in maistrie hym above."*

The tale the Wife of Bath tells about the transformation of an old hag into a beautiful maid was quite well known in folk legend and poetry. One of Chaucer's contemporaries, the poet John Gower, wrote a version of the same tale that was very popular in Chaucer's time. But whereas the moral of the folk tale of the loathsome hag is that true beauty lies within, the Wife of Bath arrives at such a conclusion only incidentally. Her message is that, ugly or fair, women should be obeyed in all things by their husbands.

The old hag might be intended to represent the Wife of Bath herself, at least as she would like others to see her. Though the hag has aged, she is capable of displaying all of the vigor and inner beauty of her youth if the right man comes along, just as the Wife did with her fifth and favorite husband, the youthful Jankyn. Although the old hag becomes a beautiful young woman in response to the young knight's well-timed response, it is unclear whether he truly had enough respect for the old woman that he allowed her to choose for herself, or whether he had simply learned how to supply her with the correct answer.

If we agree with the former, we may see the Wife as an idealistic character who believes that bad men can change. If we choose the latter, the Wife becomes a much more cynical character, inclined to mistrust all men. In the second interpretation, both transformations—the knight's shallow change in behavior (but not in soul) and the hag's transformation into the physical object of desires—are only skin deep. Perhaps she is giving him exactly what he deserves: superficiality.

The Wife begins her tale by depicting the golden age of King Arthur as one that was both more perilous and more full of opportunity for women. Every time a woman traveled alone, the Wife suggests, she was in danger of encountering an *incubus*, or an evil spirit who would seduce women (880). But the society is also highly matriarchal. After the knight commits a rape, the king hands him over to Arthur's queen, who decides to send him on an educational quest. His education comes through women, and the queen's challenge puts him in a situation where what is traditionally thought of as a shortcoming—a woman's inability to keep a secret—is the only thing that can save him. The Wife's digression about King Midas may also be slightly subversive. Instead of finishing the story, she directs the reader to Ovid. In Ovid's version of the story, the only person who knows about Midas's ass's ears is not his wife but his barber. The wife could, therefore, be slyly trying to point out that men, too, are gossips.

The Pardoner's Introduction, Prologue, and Tale

Fragment VI, lines 287–968

Summary: Introduction to the Pardoner's Tale

The Host reacts to the Physician's Tale, which has just been told. He is shocked at the death of the young Roman girl in the tale, and mourns the fact that her beauty ultimately caused the chain of events that led her father to kill her. Wanting to cheer up, the Host asks the Pardoner to tell the group a merrier, farcical tale. The

Pardoner agrees, but will continue only after he has food and drink in his stomach. Other pilgrims interject that they would prefer to hear a moral story, and the Pardoner again agrees.

SUMMARY: PROLOGUE TO THE PARDONER'S TALE

> *My theme is alwey oon, and evere was—*
> *Radix malorum est Cupiditas.*

After getting a drink, the Pardoner begins his Prologue. He tells the company about his occupation—a combination of itinerant preaching and selling promises of salvation. His sermon topic always remains the same: *Radix malorum est Cupiditas,* or "greed is the root of all evil." He gives a similar sermon to every congregation and then breaks out his bag of "relics"—which, he readily admits to the listening pilgrims, are fake. He will take a sheep's bone and claim it has miraculous healing powers for all kinds of ailments. The parishioners always believe him and make their offerings to the relics, which the Pardoner quickly pockets.

The Pardoner admits that he preaches solely to get money, not to correct sin. He argues that many sermons are the product of evil intentions. By preaching, the Pardoner can get back at anyone who has offended him or his brethren. In his sermon, he always preaches about covetousness, the very vice that he himself is gripped by. His one and only interest is to fill his ever-deepening pockets. He would rather take the last penny from a widow and her starving family than give up his money, and the good cheeses, breads, and wines that such income brings him. Speaking of alcohol, he notes, he has now finished his drink of "corny ale" and is ready to begin his tale.

SUMMARY: THE PARDONER'S TALE
The Pardoner describes a group of young Flemish people who spend their time drinking and reveling, indulging in all forms of excess. After commenting on their lifestyle of debauchery, the Pardoner enters into a tirade against the vices that they practice. First and foremost is gluttony, which he identifies as the sin that first caused the fall of mankind in Eden. Next, he attacks drunkenness, which makes a man seem mad and witless. Next is gambling, the temptation that ruins men of power and wealth. Finally, he denounces swearing. He argues that it so offends God that he forbade swearing in the Second Commandment—placing it higher up on the list than homicide. After almost two hundred lines of sermonizing, the Pardoner finally returns to his story of the lecherous Flemish youngsters.

As three of these rioters sit drinking, they hear a funeral knell. One of the revelers' servants tells the group that an old friend of theirs was slain that very night by a mysterious figure named Death. The rioters are outraged and, in their drunkenness, decide to find and kill Death to avenge their friend. Traveling down the road, they meet an old man who appears sorrowful. He says his sorrow stems from old age—he has been waiting for Death to come and take him for some time, and he has wandered all over the world. The youths, hearing the name of Death, demand to know where they can find him. The old man directs them into a grove, where he says he just left Death under an oak tree. The rioters rush to the tree, underneath which they find not Death but eight bushels of gold coins with no owner in sight.

At first, they are speechless, but, then, the slyest of the three reminds them that if they carry the gold into town in daylight, they will be taken for thieves. They must transport the gold under cover of night, and so someone must run into town to fetch bread and wine in the meantime. They draw lots, and the youngest of the three loses and runs off toward town. As soon as he is gone, the sly plotter turns to his friend and divulges his plan: when their friend returns from town, they will kill him and therefore receive greater shares of the wealth. The second rioter agrees, and they prepare their trap. Back in town, the youngest vagrant is having similar thoughts. He could easily be the richest man in town, he realizes, if he could have all the gold to himself. He goes to the apothecary and buys the strongest poison available, then puts the poison into two bottles of wine, leaving a third bottle pure for himself. He returns to the tree, but the other two rioters leap out and kill him.

They sit down to drink their friend's wine and celebrate, but each happens to pick up a poisoned bottle. Within minutes, they lie dead next to their friend. Thus, concludes the Pardoner, all must beware the sin of avarice, which can only bring treachery and death. He realizes that he has forgotten something: he has relics and pardons in his bag. According to his custom, he tells the pilgrims the value of his relics and asks for contributions—even though he has just told them the relics are fake. He offers the Host the first chance to come forth and kiss the relics, since the Host is clearly the most enveloped in sin (942). The Host is outraged and proposes to make a relic out of the Pardoner's genitals, but the Knight calms everybody down. The Host and Pardoner kiss and make up, and all have a good laugh as they continue on their way.

ANALYSIS

We know from the General Prologue that the Pardoner is as corrupt as others in his profession, but his frankness about his own hypocrisy is nevertheless shocking. He bluntly accuses himself of fraud, avarice, and gluttony—the very things he preaches against. And yet, rather than expressing any sort of remorse with his confession, he takes a perverse pride in the depth of his corruption. The Pardoner's earnestness in portraying himself as totally amoral seems almost too extreme to be accurate. His boasts about his corruption may represent his attempt to cover up his doubts or anxieties about the life of crime (in the name of religion) that he has adopted. It is possible to argue that the Pardoner sacrifices his own spiritual good to cure the sins of others. Yet he doesn't seem to really consider his spiritual corruption a real sacrifice, since he loves the money and the comforts it brings him. Either way, he quickly covers up his statement, which shows at least a flicker of interest in the good of other people, with a renewed proclamation of his own selfishness: "But that is nat my principal entente; / I preche nothyng but for coveitise" (432–433).

The Pardoner's Tale is an example, a type of story often used by preachers to emphasize a moral point to their audience. The Pardoner has told us in his Prologue that his main theme—"Greed is the root of all evil"—never changes. We can assume that the Pardoner is well practiced in the art of telling this specific tale, and he even inserts some of his sermon into it. The Pardoner's point is quite obvious—his tale shows the disastrous effects of greed. The hypocrisy he has described in his Prologue becomes evident in his tale, as all the vices he lists in his diatribe at the beginning—gluttony, drunkenness, gambling, and swearing—are faults that he himself has either displayed to the other pilgrims or proudly claimed to possess. Ridiculously, when he has finished his condemnation of swearing, he begins the tale swearing his own oath: "Now, for the love of Crist, that for us dyde . . . now wol I telle forth my tale" (658–660). Such an overtly hypocritical act is perfectly consistent with the character that the Pardoner has presented to us, and an example of Chaucer's typically wry comedy.

As if on automatic pilot, the Pardoner completes his tale just as he would when preaching in the villages, by displaying his false relics and asking for contributions. His act is intriguing, for he makes no acknowledgment of his hypocrisy. Only a few lines before, in his Prologue, he exposed to the entire company the fraudulence of his whole operation. It is inconceivable that he would now expect to get contributions from his fellow travelers—so why does he ask for them? Perhaps, like a professional actor, the Pardoner enjoys the challenge of telling his tale so convincingly that he tricks his audience into belief, even *after* he has explained to them his corrupt nature. Or perhaps he takes delight in showing the audience how his routine works, as an actor might enjoy showing people backstage. In any case, the Pardoner's attempt to sell pardons to the pilgrims is a source of rancor for the Host, because, in trying to swindle the other pilgrims, the Pardoner has violated the Host's notion of fellowship on which the storytelling pilgrimage is based.

The Nun's Priest's Prologue, Tale, and Epilogue

Fragment VII, lines 2768–3446

Summary: The Prologue of the Nun's Priest
After the Monk has told his tale, the Knight pleads that no more tragedies be told. He asks that someone tell a tale that is the opposite of tragedy, one that narrates the extreme good fortune of someone previously brought low. The Host picks the Nun's Priest, the priest traveling with the Prioress and her nun, and demands that he tell a tale that will gladden the hearts of the company members. The Nun's Priest readily agrees, and begins his tale.

Summary: The Tale of the Nun's Priest
A poor, elderly widow lives a simple life in a cottage with her two daughters. Her few possessions include three sows, three cows, a sheep, and some chickens. One chicken, her rooster, is named Chanticleer, which in French means "sings clearly." True to his name, Chanticleer's "cock-a-doodle-doo" makes him the master of all roosters. He crows the hour more accurately than any church clock. His crest is redder than fine coral, his beak is black as jet, his nails whiter than lilies, and his feathers shine like burnished gold. Understandably, such an attractive cock would have to be the Don Juan of the barnyard. Chanticleer has many hen-wives, but he loves most truly a hen named Pertelote. She is as lovely as Chanticleer is magnificent.

As Chanticleer, Pertelote, and all of Chanticleer's ancillary hen-wives are roosting one night, Chanticleer has a terrible nightmare about an orange houndlike beast who threatens to kill him while he is in the yard. Fearless Pertelote berates him for letting a dream get the better of him. She believes the dream to be the result of some physical malady, and she promises him that she will find some purgative herbs. She urges him once more not to dread something as fleeting and illusory as a dream. In order to convince her that his dream was important, he tells the stories of men who dreamed of murder and then discovered it. His point in telling these stories is to prove to Pertelote that "Mordre will out" (3052)—murder will reveal itself—even and especially in dreams. Chanticleer cites textual examples of famous dream interpretations to further support his thesis that dreams are portentous. He then praises Pertelote's beauty and grace, and the aroused hero and heroine make love in barnyard fashion: "He fethered Pertelote twenty tyme, / And trad hire eke as ofte, er it was pryme [he clasped Pertelote with his wings twenty times, and copulated with her as often, before it was 6 A.M." (3177–3178).

One day in May, Chanticleer has just declared his perfect happiness when a wave of sadness passes over him. That very night, a hungry fox stalks Chanticleer and his wives, watching their every move. The next day, Chanticleer notices the fox while watching a butterfly, and the fox confronts him with dissimulating courtesy, telling the rooster not to be afraid. Chanticleer relishes the fox's flattery of his singing. He beats his wings with pride, stands on his toes, stretches his neck, closes his eyes, and crows loudly. The fox reaches out and grabs Chanticleer by the throat, and then slinks away with him back toward the woods. No one is around to witness what has happened. Once Pertelote finds out what has happened, she burns her feathers with grief, and a great wail arises from the henhouse.

The widow and her daughters hear the screeching and spy the fox running away with the rooster. The dogs follow, and pretty soon the whole barnyard joins in the hullabaloo. Chanticleer very cleverly suggests that the fox turn and boast to his pursuers. The fox opens his mouth to do so, and Chanticleer flies out of the fox's mouth and into a high tree. The fox tries to flatter the bird into coming down, but Chanticleer has learned his lesson. He tells the fox that flattery will work for him no more. The moral of the story, concludes the Nun's Priest, is never to trust a flatterer.

SUMMARY: THE EPILOGUE TO THE NUN'S PRIEST'S TALE
The Host tells the Nun's Priest that he would have been an excellent rooster—for if he has as much courage as he has strength, he would need hens. The Host points out the Nun's Priest's strong muscles,

his great neck, and his large breast, and compares him to a sparrow-hawk. He merrily wishes the Nun's Priest good luck.

ANALYSIS

The Nun's Priest's Tale is a fable, a simple tale about animals that concludes with a moral lesson. Stylistically, however, the tale is much more complex than its simple plot would suggest. Into the fable framework, the Nun's Priest brings parodies of epic poetry, medieval scholarship, and courtly romance. Most critics are divided about whether to interpret this story as a parody or as an allegory. If viewed as a parody, the story is an ironic and humorous retelling of the fable of the fox and the rooster in the guise of, alternately, a courtly romance and a Homeric epic. It is hilariously done, since into the squawkings and struttings of poultry life, Chaucer transposes scenes of a hero's dreaming of death and courting his lady love, in a manner that imitates the overblown, descriptive style of romances. For example, the rooster's plumage is described as shining like burnished gold. He also parodies epic poetry by utilizing apostrophes, or formal, imploring addresses: "O false mordrour, lurkynge in thy den!" (3226), and "O Chauntecleer, acursed be that morwe / That thou into the yerd flaugh fro the bemes!" (3230–3231). If we read the story as an allegory, Chanticleer's story is a tale of how we are all easily swayed by the smooth, flattering tongue of the devil, represented by the fox. Other scholars have read the tale as the story of Adam and Eve's (and consequently all humankind's) fall from grace told through the veil of a fable.

The Nun's Priest's Tale is the only one of all the tales to feature a specific reference to an actual late-fourteenth-century event. This reference occurs when the widow and her daughters begin to chase the fox, and the whole barnyard screeches and bellows, joining in the fray. The narrator notes that not even the crew of Jack Straw, the reputed leader of the English peasants' rebellion in 1381, made half as much noise as did this barnyard cacophony: "Certes, he Jakke Straw and his meynee / Ne made nevere shoutes half so shrille / Whan that they wolden any Flemyng kille, / As thilke day was maad upon the fox" (3394–3397). This first and only contemporary reference in *The Canterbury Tales* dates at least the completion of the tale of Chanticleer to the 1380s, a time of great civil unrest and class turmoil.

IMPORTANT QUOTATIONS EXPLAINED

1. Whan that Aprill with his shoures soote
    The droghte of March hath perced to the roote,
    And bathed every veyne in swich licour
    Of which vertu engendred is the flour;
    Whan Zephirus eek with his sweete breeth
    Inspired hath in every holt and heeth
    The tendre croppes, and the yonge sonne
    Hath in the Ram his halve cours yronne,
    And smale fowles maken melodye,
    That slepen al the nyght with open ye
    (So priketh hem nature in hir corages),
    Thanne longen folk to goon on pilgrimages.

    (General Prologue, 1–12)

These are the opening lines with which the narrator begins the General Prologue of *The Canterbury Tales*. The imagery in this opening passage is of spring's renewal and rebirth. April's sweet showers have penetrated the dry earth of March, hydrating the roots, which in turn coax flowers out of the ground. The constellation Taurus is in the sky; Zephyr, the warm, gentle west wind, has breathed life into the fields; and the birds chirp merrily. The verbs used to describe Nature's actions—piercing (2), engendering (4), inspiring (5), and pricking (11)—conjure up images of conception.

The natural world's reawakening aligns with the narrator's similarly "inspired" poetic sensibility. The classical (Latin and Ancient Greek) authors that Chaucer emulated and wanted to surpass would always begin their epic narrative poems by invoking a muse, or female goddess, to inspire them, quite literally to talk or breathe a story into them. Most of them begin "Sing in me, O muse," about a particular subject. Chaucer too begins with a moment of inspiration, but in this case it is the natural inspiration of the earth readying itself for spring rather than a supernatural being filling the poet's body with her voice.

After the long sleep of winter, people begin to stir, feeling the need to "goon on pilgrimages," or to travel to a site where one worships a saint's relics as a means of spiritual cleansing and renewal. Since winter ice and snow made traveling long distances almost impossible (this was an age not only before automobiles but also before adequately developed horse-drawn carriages), the need to get up, stretch one's legs, and see the world outside the window must have been great. Pilgrimages combined spring vacations with religious purification.

The landscape in this passage also clearly situates the text in England. This is not a classical landscape like the Troy of Homer's *Iliad,* nor is it an entirely fictionalized space like the cool groves and rocky cliffs of imaginary Arcadia from pastoral poetry and romances. Chaucer's landscape is also accessible to all types of people, but especially those who inhabit the countryside, since Chaucer speaks of budding flowers, growing crops, and singing birds.

QUOTATIONS

2.   The Firste Moevere of the cause above,
       Whan he first made the faire cheyne of love,
       Greet was th'effect, and heigh was his entente.
       . . .
       For with that faire cheyne of love he bond
       The fyr, the eyr, the water, and the lond
       In certeyn boundes, that they may nat flee.
                                    (The Knight's Tale, 2987–2993)

This passage is from the conclusion of the Knight's Tale, as Duke Theseus explains why Emelye must marry the knight Palamon. Theseus bases his argument on concepts drawn from the fifth-century A.D. Roman philosopher Boethius, whose ideas appealed to medieval Christians because he combined Plato's theory of an ideal world with Christian teachings of a moral universe. Chaucer took it upon himself to translate and provide a commentary for Boethius's *Consolation of Philosophy*. Chaucer's translation, a long prose text, is informally known as his *Boece*.

The "Firste Moevere" (first mover) is the Aristotelian notion of God. The story the Knight tells takes place long before Christ. Although medieval Christians could not condemn classical writers and philosophers, since much of Virgil's poetry and Plato's philosophy formed the basis for Christian literature, they had difficulty imagining a time before people believed in Christ. Chaucer (or the Knight) has carefully given Theseus a pagan notion of God that nevertheless resonates with Christianity. Having a supreme ancient Greek or Roman god would be idolatrous and therefore immoral (although the gods appear as lesser entities in the second half of the tale), because, according to medieval Christians, there was only one god and that god was the Trinity.

The "faire cheyne of love" is a medieval view of cosmology, or the natural order of things. It is the idea that every thing has its place in the hierarchy of the world, from the smallest flea to the hand of God. The fifty lines or so that follow this passage contain ideas that are taken almost word for word from Chaucer's *Boece*. Theseus argues that Emelye's overly long mourning threatens to disrupt the great chain of love, and that the only way to maintain the chain's balance is for her to marry Palamon and be happy.

QUOTATIONS

3.　　Thus swyved was this carpenteris wyf,
　　　For al his kepyng and his jalousye;
　　　And Absolon hath kist hir nether ye;
　　　And Nicholas is scalded in the towte.
　　　This tale is doon, and God save al the rowte!

(The Miller's Tale, 3850–3854)

This passage, the rhyming conclusion to the Miller's Tale, neatly resolves the story by offering a reckoning of accounts. Everyone in the story has learned his or her lesson and gotten the physical punishment he or she deserves. The carpenter's wife, Alisoun, was "swyved," or possessed in bed by another man, in this case, Nicholas. John, the ignorant and jealous carpenter, has been made a cuckold, despite his watchful and possessive eye. Absolon, the foolish and foppish parish clerk, has kissed Alisoun's behind, fair punishment for evading his clerical duties. Nicholas, the smart-alecky student who cheated on the carpenter with Alisoun, has been burned on his bottom with a red-hot poker as payback for farting in Absolon's face. Still, the distribution of punishments is not entirely equal. John is dealt the worst lot—he ends up with a broken arm and the whole town believing he has gone insane. Alisoun's "swyving" is a double punishment for John, while Alisoun herself escapes unscathed.

KEY FACTS

FULL TITLE
The Canterbury Tales

AUTHOR
Geoffrey Chaucer

TYPE OF WORK
Poetry (two tales are in prose: the Tale of Melibee and the
Parson's Tale)

GENRES
Narrative collection of poems; character portraits; parody;
estates satire; romance; fabliau

LANGUAGE
Middle English

TIME AND PLACE WRITTEN
Around 1386–1395, England

DATE OF FIRST PUBLICATION
Sometime in the early fifteenth century

PUBLISHER
Originally circulated in hand-copied manuscripts

NARRATOR
The primary narrator is an anonymous, naïve member of the
pilgrimage, who is not described. The other pilgrims narrate
most of the tales.

POINT OF VIEW
In the General Prologue, the narrator speaks in the first person,
describing each of the pilgrims as they appeared to him. Though
narrated by different pilgrims, each of the tales is told from an
omniscient third-person point of view, providing the reader
with the thoughts as well as actions of the characters.

TONE
The Canterbury Tales incorporates an impressive range of
attitudes toward life and literature. The tales are by turns
satirical, elevated, pious, earthy, bawdy, and comical. The

reader should not accept the naïve narrator's point of view
as Chaucer's.

TENSE

Past

SETTING (TIME)

The late fourteenth century, after 1381

SETTING (PLACE)

The Tabard Inn; the road to Canterbury

PROTAGONISTS

Each individual tale has protagonists, but Chaucer's plan is to
make none of his storytellers superior to others; it is an equal
company. In the Knight's Tale, the protagonists are Palamon
and Arcite; in the Miller's Tale, Nicholas and Alisoun; in the
Wife of Bath's Tale, the errant knight and the loathsome hag; in
the Nun's Priest's Tale, the rooster Chanticleer.

MAJOR CONFLICT

The struggles between characters, manifested in the links
between tales, mostly involve clashes between social classes,
differing tastes, and competing professions. There are also
clashes between the sexes, and there is resistance to the Host's
somewhat tyrannical leadership.

RISING ACTION

As he sets off on a pilgrimage to Canterbury, the narrator
encounters a group of other pilgrims and joins them. That
night, the Host of the tavern where the pilgrims are staying
presents them with a storytelling challenge and appoints himself
judge of the competition and leader of the company.

CLIMAX

Not applicable (collection of tales)

FALLING ACTION

After twenty-three tales have been told, the Parson delivers
a long sermon. Chaucer then makes a retraction, asking
to be forgiven for his sins, including having written *The
Canterbury Tales*.

THEMES
The pervasiveness of courtly love, the importance of company, the corruption of the church

MOTIFS
Romance, fabliaux

SYMBOLS
Springtime, clothing, physiognomy

FORESHADOWING
Not applicable (collection of tales)

KEY FACTS

STUDY QUESTIONS

1. *Why is the Knight first in the General Prologue and first to tell a tale?*

The Knight is first to be described in the General Prologue because he is the highest on the social scale, being closest to belonging to the highest estate, the aristocracy. The Knight's nobility derives from the courtly and Christian values he has sworn to uphold: truth, honor, freedom, and courtesy. The Knight's Tale comes first because he has drawn the shortest straw of the group, although the narrator's comment that the Knight drew the shortest straw "[were] it by aventure, or sort, or cas [whether by chance, luck, or destiny]" seems to suggest that he feels that it was *not* by chance at all that the Knight tells his tale first (General Prologue, 844).

2. *What makes the Pardoner so offensive?*

The Pardoner is the most controversial of all the pilgrims for four reasons: his work, his sin (greed), his unrepentant pride, and his sexuality. The Pardoner's job—giving people written absolution from sin—was a dubious profession in medieval Europe. As he reveals in his Prologue, the Pardoner is well aware that he himself is covetous, which is the very sin against which he preaches in order to con people into giving him money. What makes him so distasteful to the other characters, especially the Host, is that fact that he is so proud of his vice. In the General Prologue, the narrator suggests that the Pardoner's sexual orientation is ambiguous, which means that he occupies an even further marginalized position in fourteenth-century society.

How to Write
Literary Analysis

The Literary Essay: A Step-by-Step Guide

When you read for pleasure, your only goal is enjoyment. You might find yourself reading to get caught up in an exciting story, to learn about an interesting time or place, or just to pass time. Maybe you're looking for inspiration, guidance, or a reflection of your own life. There are as many different, valid ways of reading a book as there are books in the world.

When you read a work of literature in an English class, however, you're being asked to read in a special way: you're being asked to perform *literary analysis*. To analyze something means to break it down into smaller parts and then examine how those parts work, both individually and together. Literary analysis involves examining all the parts of a novel, play, short story, or poem—elements such as character, setting, tone, and imagery—and thinking about how the author uses those elements to create certain effects.

A literary essay isn't a book review: you're not being asked whether or not you liked a book or whether you'd recommend it to another reader. A literary essay also isn't like the kind of book report you wrote when you were younger, where your teacher wanted you to summarize the book's action. A high school- or college-level literary essay asks, "How does this piece of literature actually work?" "How does it do what it does?" and, "Why might the author have made the choices he or she did?"

The Seven Steps

No one is born knowing how to analyze literature; it's a skill you learn and a process you can master. As you gain more practice with this kind of thinking and writing, you'll be able to craft a method that works best for you. But until then, here are seven basic steps to writing a well-constructed literary essay:

1. *Ask questions*
2. *Collect evidence*
3. *Construct a thesis*

4. *Develop and organize arguments*
5. *Write the introduction*
6. *Write the body paragraphs*
7. *Write the conclusion*

1. ASK QUESTIONS

When you're assigned a literary essay in class, your teacher will often provide you with a list of writing prompts. Lucky you! Now all you have to do is choose one. Do yourself a favor and pick a topic that interests you. You'll have a much better (not to mention easier) time if you start off with something you enjoy thinking about. If you are asked to come up with a topic by yourself, though, you might start to feel a little panicked. Maybe you have too many ideas—or none at all. Don't worry. Take a deep breath and start by asking yourself these questions:

- **What struck you?** Did a particular image, line, or scene linger in your mind for a long time? If it fascinated you, chances are you can draw on it to write a fascinating essay.

- **What confused you?** Maybe you were surprised to see a character act in a certain way, or maybe you didn't understand why the book ended the way it did. Confusing moments in a work of literature are like a loose thread in a sweater: if you pull on it, you can unravel the entire thing. Ask yourself why the author chose to write about that character or scene the way he or she did and you might tap into some important insights about the work as a whole.

- **Did you notice any patterns?** Is there a phrase that the main character uses constantly or an image that repeats throughout the book? If you can figure out how that pattern weaves through the work and what the significance of that pattern is, you've almost got your entire essay mapped out.

- **Did you notice any contradictions or ironies?** Great works of literature are complex; great literary essays recognize and explain those complexities. Maybe the title (*Happy Days*) totally disagrees with the book's subject matter (hungry orphans dying in the woods). Maybe the main character acts one way around his family and a completely different way around his friends and associates. If you can find a way to explain a work's contradictory elements, you've got the seeds of a great essay.

At this point, you don't need to know exactly what you're going to say about your topic; you just need a place to begin your exploration. You can help direct your reading and brainstorming by formulating your topic as a *question,* which you'll then try to answer in your essay. The best questions invite critical debates and discussions, not just a rehashing of the summary. Remember, you're looking for something you can *prove or argue* based on evidence you find in the text. Finally, remember to keep the scope of your question in mind: is this a topic you can adequately address within the word or page limit you've been given? Conversely, is this a topic big enough to fill the required length?

GOOD QUESTIONS
"Are Romeo and Juliet's parents responsible for the deaths of their children?"
"Why do pigs keep showing up in LORD OF THE FLIES?*"*
"Are Dr. Frankenstein and his monster alike? How?"

BAD QUESTIONS
"What happens to Scout in TO KILL A MOCKINGBIRD?*"*
"What do the other characters in JULIUS CAESAR *think about Caesar?"*
"How does Hester Prynne in THE SCARLET LETTER *remind me of my sister?"*

---

2. COLLECT EVIDENCE
Once you know what question you want to answer, it's time to scour the book for things that will help you answer the question. Don't worry if you don't know what you want to say yet—right now you're just collecting ideas and material and letting it all percolate. Keep track of passages, symbols, images, or scenes that deal with your topic. Eventually, you'll start making connections between these examples and your thesis will emerge.

Here's a brief summary of the various parts that compose each and every work of literature. These are the elements that you will analyze in your essay, and which you will offer as evidence to support your arguments. For more on the parts of literary works, see the Glossary of Literary Terms at the end of this section.

LITERARY ANALYSIS

ELEMENTS OF STORY   These are the *what*s of the work—what happens, where it happens, and to whom it happens.

- **Plot:** All of the events and actions of the work.
- **Character:** The people who act and are acted upon in a literary work. The main character of a work is known as the *protagonist.*
- **Conflict:** The central tension in the work. In most cases, the protagonist wants something, while opposing forces (antagonists) hinder the protagonist's progress.
- **Setting:** When and where the work takes place. Elements of setting include location, time period, time of day, weather, social atmosphere, and economic conditions.
- **Narrator:** The person telling the story. The narrator may straightforwardly report what happens, convey the subjective opinions and perceptions of one or more characters, or provide commentary and opinion in his or her own voice.
- **Themes:** The main idea or message of the work—usually an abstract idea about people, society, or life in general. A work may have many themes, which may be in tension with one another.

ELEMENTS OF STYLE   These are the *how*s—how the characters speak, how the story is constructed, and how language is used throughout the work.

- **Structure and organization:** How the parts of the work are assembled. Some novels are narrated in a linear, chronological fashion, while others skip around in time. Some plays follow a traditional three- or five-act structure, while others are a series of loosely connected scenes. Some authors deliberately leave gaps in their works, leaving readers to puzzle out the missing information. A work's structure and organization can tell you a lot about the kind of message it wants to convey.
- **Point of view:** The perspective from which a story is told. In *first-person point of view,* the narrator involves him or herself in the story. ("I went to the store"; "We watched in horror as the bird slammed into the window.") A first-person narrator is usually the protagonist of the work, but not always. In *third-person point of view,* the narrator does not participate

in the story. A third-person narrator may closely follow a
specific character, recounting that individual character's
thoughts or experiences, or it may be what we call an
omniscient narrator. Omniscient narrators see and know all:
they can witness any event in any time or place and are privy
to the inner thoughts and feelings of all characters. Remember
that the narrator and the author are not the same thing!

- **Diction:** Word choice. Whether a character uses dry, clinical
  language or flowery prose with lots of exclamation points
  can tell you a lot about his or her attitude and personality.

- **Syntax:** Word order and sentence construction. Syntax is
  a crucial part of establishing an author's narrative voice.
  Ernest Hemingway, for example, is known for writing in
  very short, straightforward sentences, while James Joyce
  characteristically wrote in long, incredibly complicated lines.

- **Tone:** The mood or feeling of the text. Diction and syntax
  often contribute to the tone of a work. A novel written in
  short, clipped sentences that use small, simple words might
  feel brusque, cold, or matter-of-fact.

- **Imagery:** Language that appeals to the senses, representing
  things that can be seen, smelled, heard, tasted, or touched.

- **Figurative language:** Language that is not meant to be
  interpreted literally. The most common types of figurative
  language are *metaphors* and *similes,* which compare two
  unlike things in order to suggest a similarity between them—
  for example, "All the world's a stage," or "The moon is like
  a ball of green cheese." (Metaphors say one thing *is* another
  thing; similes claim that one thing is *like* another thing.)

---

3. CONSTRUCT A THESIS

When you've examined all the evidence you've collected and know
how you want to answer the question, it's time to write your thesis
statement. A *thesis* is a claim about a work of literature that needs to
be supported by evidence and arguments. The thesis statement is the
heart of the literary essay, and the bulk of your paper will be spent
trying to prove this claim. A good thesis will be:

- **Arguable**. "*The Great Gatsby* describes New York society in
  the 1920s" isn't a thesis—it's a fact.

- **Provable through textual evidence**. "*Hamlet* is a confusing but ultimately very well-written play" is a weak thesis because it offers the writer's personal opinion about the book. Yes, it's arguable, but it's not a claim that can be proved or supported with examples taken from the play itself.

- **Surprising**. "Both George and Lenny change a great deal in *Of Mice and Men*" is a weak thesis because it's obvious. A really strong thesis will argue for a reading of the text that is not immediately apparent.

- **Specific.** "Dr. Frankenstein's monster tells us a lot about the human condition" is *almost* a really great thesis statement, but it's still too vague. What does the writer mean by "a lot"? *How* does the monster tell us so much about the human condition?

GOOD THESIS STATEMENTS

Question: In *Romeo and Juliet*, which is more powerful in shaping the lovers' story: fate or foolishness?

Thesis: "Though Shakespeare defines Romeo and Juliet as 'star-crossed lovers' and images of stars and planets appear throughout the play, a closer examination of that celestial imagery reveals that the stars are merely witnesses to the characters' foolish activities and not the causes themselves."

Question: How does the bell jar function as a symbol in Sylvia Plath's *The Bell Jar*?

Thesis: "A bell jar is a bell-shaped glass that has three basic uses: to hold a specimen for observation, to contain gases, and to maintain a vacuum. The bell jar appears in each of these capacities in *The Bell Jar,* Plath's semi-autobiographical novel, and each appearance marks a different stage in Esther's mental breakdown."

Question: Would Piggy in *The Lord of the Flies* make a good island leader if he were given the chance?

Thesis: "Though the intelligent, rational, and innovative Piggy has the mental characteristics of a good leader, he ultimately lacks the social skills necessary to be an effective one. Golding emphasizes this point by giving Piggy a foil in the charismatic Jack, whose magnetic personality allows him to capture and wield power effectively, if not always wisely."

4. Develop and Organize Arguments

The reasons and examples that support your thesis will form the middle paragraphs of your essay. Since you can't really write your thesis statement until you know how you'll structure your argument, you'll probably end up working on steps 3 and 4 at the same time.

There's no single method of argumentation that will work in every context. One essay prompt might ask you to compare and contrast two characters, while another asks you to trace an image through a given work of literature. These questions require different kinds of answers and therefore different kinds of arguments. Below, we'll discuss three common kinds of essay prompts and some strategies for constructing a solid, well-argued case.

Types of Literary Essays

- **Compare and contrast**

  Compare and contrast the characters of Huck and Jim in The Adventures of Huckleberry Finn.

  Chances are you've written this kind of essay before. In an academic literary context, you'll organize your arguments the same way you would in any other class. You can either go *subject by subject* or *point by point*. In the former, you'll discuss one character first and then the second. In the latter, you'll choose several traits (attitude toward life, social status, images and metaphors associated with the character) and devote a paragraph to each. You may want to use a mix of these two approaches—for example, you may want to spend a paragraph a piece broadly sketching Huck's and Jim's personalities before transitioning into a paragraph or two that describes a few key points of comparison. This can be a highly effective strategy if you want to make a counterintuitive argument—that, despite seeming to be totally different, the two objects being compared are actually similar in a very important way (or vice versa). Remember that your essay should reveal something fresh or unexpected about the text, so think beyond the obvious parallels and differences.

- **Trace**

  Choose an image—for example, birds, knives, or eyes—and trace that image throughout Macbeth.

  Sounds pretty easy, right? All you need to do is read the play, underline every appearance of a knife in *Macbeth*, and then list them in your essay in the order they appear, right? Well, not exactly. Your teacher doesn't want a simple catalog of examples. He or she wants to see you make *connections* between those examples—that's the difference between summarizing and analyzing. In the *Macbeth* example above, think about the different contexts in which knives appear in the play and to what effect. In *Macbeth,* there are real knives and imagined knives; knives that kill and knives that simply threaten. Categorize and classify your examples to give them some order. Finally, always keep the overall effect in mind. After you choose and analyze your examples, you should come to some greater understanding about the work, as well as your chosen image, symbol, or phrase's role in developing the major themes and stylistic strategies of that work.

- **Debate**

  Is the society depicted in 1984 good for its citizens?

  In this kind of essay, you're being asked to debate a moral, ethical, or aesthetic issue regarding the work. You might be asked to judge a character or group of characters (*Is Caesar responsible for his own demise?*) or the work itself (*Is* JANE EYRE *a feminist novel?*). For this kind of essay, there are two important points to keep in mind. First, don't simply base your arguments on your personal feelings and reactions. Every literary essay expects you to read and analyze the work, so search for evidence in the text. What do characters in *1984* have to say about the government of Oceania? What images does Orwell use that might give you a hint about his attitude toward the government? As in any debate, you also need to make sure that you define all the necessary terms before you begin to argue your case. What does it mean to be a "good" society? What makes a novel "feminist"? You should define your terms right up front, in the first paragraph after your introduction.

  Second, remember that strong literary essays make contrary and surprising arguments. Try to think outside the box. In the *1984* example above, it seems like the obvious answer would be no, the totalitarian society depicted in Orwell's novel is *not* good for its citizens. But can you think of any arguments for the opposite side? Even if your final assertion is that the novel depicts a cruel, repressive, and therefore harmful society, acknowledging and responding to the counterargument will strengthen your overall case.

5. Write the Introduction

Your introduction sets up the entire essay. It's where you present your topic and articulate the particular issues and questions you'll be addressing. It's also where you, as the writer, introduce yourself to your readers. A persuasive literary essay immediately establishes its writer as a knowledgeable, authoritative figure.

An introduction can vary in length depending on the overall length of the essay, but in a traditional five-paragraph essay it should be no longer than one paragraph. However long it is, your introduction needs to:

- **Provide any necessary context.** Your introduction should situate the reader and let him or her know what to expect. What book are you discussing? Which characters? What topic will you be addressing?

- **Answer the "So what?" question.** Why is this topic important, and why is your particular position on the topic noteworthy? Ideally, your introduction should pique the reader's interest by suggesting how your argument is surprising or otherwise counterintuitive. Literary essays make unexpected connections and reveal less-than-obvious truths.

- **Present your thesis.** This usually happens at or very near the end of your introduction.

- **Indicate the shape of the essay to come.** Your reader should finish reading your introduction with a good sense of the scope of your essay as well as the path you'll take toward proving your thesis. You don't need to spell out every step, but you do need to suggest the organizational pattern you'll be using.

Your introduction should not:

- **Be vague.** Beware of the two killer words in literary analysis: *interesting* and *important*. Of course the work, question, or example is interesting and important—that's why you're writing about it!

- **Open with any grandiose assertions.** Many student readers think that beginning their essays with a flamboyant statement such as, "Since the dawn of time, writers have been fascinated with the topic of free will," makes them sound important and commanding. You know what? It actually sounds pretty amateurish.

- **Wildly praise the work.** Another typical mistake student writers make is extolling the work or author. Your teacher doesn't need to be told that "Shakespeare is perhaps the greatest writer in the English language." You can mention a work's reputation in passing—by referring to *The Adventures of Huckleberry Finn* as "Mark Twain's enduring classic," for example—but don't make a point of bringing it up unless that reputation is key to your argument.

- **Go off-topic.** Keep your introduction streamlined and to the point. Don't feel the need to throw in all kinds of bells and whistles in order to impress your reader—just get to the point as quickly as you can, without skimping on any of the required steps.

6. WRITE THE BODY PARAGRAPHS

Once you've written your introduction, you'll take the arguments you developed in step 4 and turn them into your body paragraphs. The organization of this middle section of your essay will largely be determined by the argumentative strategy you use, but no matter how you arrange your thoughts, your body paragraphs need to do the following:

- **Begin with a strong topic sentence.** Topic sentences are like signs on a highway: they tell the reader where they are and where they're going. A good topic sentence not only alerts readers to what issue will be discussed in the following paragraph but also gives them a sense of what argument will be made *about* that issue. "Rumor and gossip play an important role in *The Crucible*" isn't a strong topic sentence because it doesn't tell us very much. "The community's constant gossiping creates an environment that allows false accusations to flourish" is a much stronger topic sentence— it not only tells us *what* the paragraph will discuss (gossip) but *how* the paragraph will discuss the topic (by showing how gossip creates a set of conditions that leads to the play's climactic action).

- **Fully and completely develop a single thought.** Don't skip around in your paragraph or try to stuff in too much material. Body paragraphs are like bricks: each individual one needs to be strong and sturdy or the entire structure will collapse. Make sure you have really proven your point before moving on to the next one.

- **Use transitions effectively.** Good literary essay writers know that each paragraph must be clearly and strongly linked to the material around it. Think of each paragraph as a response to the one that precedes it. Use transition words and phrases such as *however, similarly, on the contrary, therefore,* and *furthermore* to indicate what kind of response you're making.

---

7. WRITE THE CONCLUSION

Just as you used the introduction to ground your readers in the topic before providing your thesis, you'll use the conclusion to quickly summarize the specifics learned thus far and then hint at the broader implications of your topic. A good conclusion will:

- **Do more than simply restate the thesis.** If your thesis argued that *The Catcher in the Rye* can be read as a Christian allegory, don't simply end your essay by saying, "And that is why *The Catcher in the Rye* can be read as a Christian allegory." If you've constructed your arguments well, this kind of statement will just be redundant.

- **Synthesize the arguments, not summarize them.** Similarly, don't repeat the details of your body paragraphs in your conclusion. The reader has already read your essay, and chances are it's not so long that they've forgotten all your points by now.

- **Revisit the "So what?" question.** In your introduction, you made a case for why your topic and position are important. You should close your essay with the same sort of gesture. What do your readers know now that they didn't know before? How will that knowledge help them better appreciate or understand the work overall?

- **Move from the specific to the general.** Your essay has most likely treated a very specific element of the work—a single character, a small set of images, or a particular passage. In your conclusion, try to show how this narrow discussion has wider implications for the work overall. If your essay on *To Kill a Mockingbird* focused on the character of Boo Radley, for example, you might want to include a bit in your conclusion about how he fits into the novel's larger message about childhood, innocence, or family life.

- **Stay relevant.** Your conclusion should suggest new directions of thought, but it shouldn't be treated as an opportunity to pad your essay with all the extra, interesting ideas you came up with during your brainstorming sessions but couldn't fit into the essay proper. Don't attempt to stuff in unrelated queries or too many abstract thoughts.

- **Avoid making overblown closing statements.** A conclusion should open up your highly specific, focused discussion, but it should do so without drawing a sweeping lesson about life or human nature. Making such observations may be part of the point of reading, but it's almost always a mistake in essays, where these observations tend to sound overly dramatic or simply silly.

A+ Essay Checklist

Congratulations! If you've followed all the steps we've outlined above, you should have a solid literary essay to show for all your efforts. What if you've got your sights set on an A+? To write the kind of superlative essay that will be rewarded with a perfect grade, keep the following rubric in mind. These are the qualities that teachers expect to see in a truly A+ essay. How does yours stack up?

✓ Demonstrates a thorough understanding of the book

✓ Presents an original, compelling argument

✓ Thoughtfully analyzes the text's formal elements

✓ Uses appropriate and insightful examples

✓ Structures ideas in a logical and progressive order

✓ Demonstrates a mastery of sentence construction, transitions, grammar, spelling, and word choice

Suggested Essay Topics

1. *Compare the Miller's Tale with either the Reeve's Tale or the Summoner's Tale. What are the different characteristics that make each tale a fabliau? Consider comic timing, plot intricacy, and the cast of characters within the tale.*

2. *Is the Wife of Bath meant to contradict the misogynist (woman-hating) ideas of her time, or to uphold them? Use the text to back up your argument.*

3. *How does Chaucer conceive of ancient history and belief systems in the Knight's Tale? How is his vision anachronistic? How does he attempt to make it less so? What is the function of time and the seasons in the tale?*

A+ Student Essay

> Courtly love is a recurring theme in *The Canterbury Tales*.
> How does the concept of courtly love develop over the
> course of the book? Focus your discussion on three tales.

Courtly love was one of the most pervasive themes in the literature
of Chaucer's time. According to this conception of love, romance
is an ennobling force that can raise the male lover—usually a
knight—to heights of bravery in the service of his lady. The beloved,
in turn, is the epitome of feminine perfection and often difficult, if
not impossible, to attain as a romantic partner. Passion and devotion are emphasized throughout, and the spiritual dimension of love
is valued above the physical. The entire courtly love relationship
is figured in a heavily stylized and idealized manner according to
an established model. While Chaucer presents a fairly traditional
picture of courtly love at the beginning of the Knight's Tale, he goes
on to deconstruct the concept by introducing elements of jealousy,
gender conflict, and lust as the various tales progress. By the end
of the Nun's Priest's Tale, it is clear that, as an idealized concept,
courtly love cannot be applied to relationships where real human
emotions are concerned.

The Knight's Tale presents ideal characters for a story of courtly
love. Chaucer draws on pastoral and divine imagery to present
Emelye as the perfectly feminine love object, comparing her beauty
to fresh May flowers and her singing to that of heavenly angels.
Palamon is a royal knight who feels as if he is pierced in the heart
when he sees Emelye. The knight pining for the beautiful maiden fits
the conventions of courtly love exactly; however, Chaucer refuses
to make this a straightforward tale. Rather than battle beasts or
foreign enemies to win his lady, as we might expect, Palamon must
instead fight his closest friend, Arcite. The duel ends with Arcite's
death, which leaves Palamon and Emelye despondent over the loss
rather than happy that they are finally united. While the Knight's
Tale features highly conventional players, it refuses to let the concept of courtly love exist in a vacuum. Rather, the tale shows how
love can inspire jealousy, which can lead unexpectedly to violence
and sorrow.

The Wife of Bath's Tale moves us further away from an idealized
depiction of courtly love. Here too are knights and fair maidens, but

they are hardly the conventional archetypes. The knight in this tale is not a noble man, but a rogue: The first action we see him engage in is the rape of a young woman. Likewise, the fair maidens in the tale are far from chaste, as friars and, presumably, men such as the knight routinely molest and/or rape them. These are not honorable players engaging in the stylized rituals of courtly love. Indeed, love of the transcendent, elevating variety plays little role in this tale, as power is revealed to be the true object both men and women desire. The knight, who dominates a woman by raping her, ultimately finds that what women want most is to dominate their own mates. This illuminates the dark side of the courtly love model, in which the knight is seen as the lady's servant and she his mistress. The Wife of Bath's tale is true to the underlying power dynamics of this conventional relationship—a notion that is strengthened by the presence of an authoritative female monarch who directs a submissive knight—but in this context those elements seem far from noble or admirable.

Finally, the Nun's Priest's Tale presents a comic parody of courtly love, set in a most atypical setting. In an old widow's barnyard, we are introduced to a magnificent cock named Chanticleer who loves a "faire damoysele," the hen Pertelote. Though they are personified as the kind of handsome man and lovely maiden who might engage in the rituals of courtly love, Chaucer quickly turns our attention to their animalistic lust. Chanticleer has seven wives, and Pertelote willfully submits to him as he "fethere[s]" her "twenty tyme / And trad[s] hir eke as offe" (411–412). This image of the two fiercely and busily copulating directly counters a central tenet of courtly love, in which the spiritual element of romance is valued above the physical or erotic. Chanticleer and Pertelote go on to spend most of the tale either copulating or arguing with one another. These birds don't have the idealized love of Palamon and Emelye or the dramatic power struggle between the knight and the women in the Wife's Tale, but rather a "real" marriage, with all its imperfections. The domestic setting enhances the notion that this is an ordinary, everyday union.

As the pilgrims tell their tales, Chaucer progressively proves that the tropes and conventions of courtly love are not useful tools for describing real relationships between complex people. In this way, Chaucer's treatment of courtly love mirrors his larger project: to move literature away from fairy tales or idealized narratives toward simply presented stories of ordinary people, told in their own, everyday language.

GLOSSARY OF LITERARY TERMS

ANTAGONIST

The entity that acts to frustrate the goals of the *protagonist.* The antagonist is usually another *character* but may also be a non-human force.

ANTIHERO / ANTIHEROINE

A *protagonist* who is not admirable or who challenges notions of what should be considered admirable.

CHARACTER

A person, animal, or any other thing with a personality that appears in a *narrative.*

CLIMAX

The moment of greatest intensity in a text or the major turning point in the *plot.*

CONFLICT

The central struggle that moves the *plot* forward. The conflict can be the *protagonist*'s struggle against fate, nature, society, or another person.

FIRST-PERSON POINT OF VIEW

A literary style in which the *narrator* tells the story from his or her own *point of view* and refers to himself or herself as "I." The narrator may be an active participant in the story or just an observer.

HERO / HEROINE

The principal *character* in a literary work or *narrative.*

IMAGERY

Language that brings to mind sense-impressions, representing things that can be seen, smelled, heard, tasted, or touched.

MOTIF

A recurring idea, structure, contrast, or device that develops or informs the major *themes* of a work of literature.

NARRATIVE

A story.

NARRATOR

The person (sometimes a *character*) who tells a story; the *voice* assumed by the writer. The narrator and the author of the work of literature are not the same person.

PLOT

The arrangement of the events in a story, including the sequence in which they are told, the relative emphasis they are given, and the causal connections between events.

POINT OF VIEW

The *perspective* that a *narrative* takes toward the events it describes.

PROTAGONIST

The main *character* around whom the story revolves.

SETTING

The location of a *narrative* in time and space. Setting creates mood or atmosphere.

SUBPLOT

A secondary *plot* that is of less importance to the overall story but may serve as a point of contrast or comparison to the main plot.

SYMBOL

An object, *character,* figure, or color that is used to represent an abstract idea or concept. Unlike an *emblem,* a symbol may have different meanings in different contexts.

SYNTAX

The way the words in a piece of writing are put together to form lines, phrases, or clauses; the basic structure of a piece of writing.

THEME

A fundamental and universal idea explored in a literary work.

TONE

The author's attitude toward the subject or *characters* of a story or poem or toward the reader.

VOICE

An author's individual way of using language to reflect his or her own personality and attitudes. An author communicates voice through *tone, diction,* and *syntax.*

LITERARY ANALYSIS

A Note on Plagiarism

Plagiarism—presenting someone else's work as your own—rears its ugly head in many forms. Many students know that copying text without citing it is unacceptable. But some don't realize that even if you're not quoting directly, but instead are paraphrasing or summarizing, *it is plagiarism* unless you cite the source.

Here are the most common forms of plagiarism:

- Using an author's phrases, sentences, or paragraphs without citing the source
- Paraphrasing an author's ideas without citing the source
- Passing off another student's work as your own

How do you steer clear of plagiarism? You should *always* acknowledge all words and ideas that aren't your own by using quotation marks around verbatim text or citations like footnotes and endnotes to note another writer's ideas. For more information on how to give credit when credit is due, ask your teacher for guidance or visit www.sparknotes.com.

Review & Resources

Quiz

1. Why are the pilgrims going to Canterbury?

   A. To meet King Henry III
   B. To see a medieval mystery play
   C. To worship the relics of Saint Thomas Becket
   D. Because they are tourists

2. What does the Squire wear?

   A. A velvet doublet and hose
   B. Cloth embroidered with flowers
   C. Green and peacock-blue hunting gear
   D. A beaver hat

3. Who marries Emelye in the Knight's Tale?

   A. Theseus
   B. Arcite
   C. Saturn
   D. Palamon

4. According to the Wife of Bath, what do women most desire?

   A. Sovereignty over their husbands
   B. True love
   C. Perfect beauty
   D. Great wealth

5. What does Chanticleer dream?

   A. That he will be killed by a wolf
   B. That Pertelote will desert him
   C. That he will be taken away by an orange, houndlike creature
   D. That his friend will be murdered

6.   Who are the three men searching for in the Pardoner's Tale?

    A.   The Wandering Jew
    B.   Greed
    C.   Jesus Christ
    D.   Death

7.   Who is branded by a red-hot poker in the Miller's Tale?

    A.   Absolon
    B.   Alisoun
    C.   Nicholas
    D.   John

8.   Which of the following tales is a fabliau?

    A.   The Knight's Tale
    B.   The Nun's Priest's Tale
    C.   The Wife of Bath's Tale
    D.   The Miller's Tale

9.   Which pilgrim has a forked beard?

    A.   The Summoner
    B.   The Merchant
    C.   The Reeve
    D.   The Physician

10.   What is the moral of the Nun's Priest's Tale?

    A.   Slow and easy wins the race.
    B.   Greed is the root of all evil.
    C.   Beauty lies within.
    D.   Never trust a flatterer.

11.   What is the Wife of Bath's Prologue about?

    A.   Her life with her five different husbands
    B.   Ovid's Metamorphoses
    C.   How women deserve to hold high public offices just
            like men
    D.   A philosophical treatise on the astrolabe

12. When does *The Canterbury Tales* take place?

   A. In the Renaissance
   B. In pre-Christian Britain
   C. During the Norman invasion
   D. In the late fourteenth century

13. For which social classes did Chaucer write?

   A. The nobility
   B. All levels of society
   C. Illiterate peasants
   D. Merchants

14. What was Chaucer's profession?

   A. Poet
   B. Noble
   C. Merchant
   D. Civil servant

15. How many Canterbury Tales are there?

   A. 80
   B. 24
   C. 16
   D. 50

16. What is a romance?

   A. An erotic tale of love and passion
   B. A story about Romans
   C. A story of knights, ladies, quests, and love
   D. A cheap book from a drugstore

17. Which tale qualifies as part of a medieval sermon?

   A. The Wife of Bath's Tale
   B. The Tale of Melibee
   C. The Physician's Tale
   D. The Pardoner's Tale

REVIEW & RESOURCES

18. Which pilgrims are most richly attired?

    A.   Miller, Yeoman, Summoner, Chaucer

    B.   Wife of Bath, Squire, Monk, Physician, Franklin

    C.   Knight, Nun's Priest, Parson, Pardoner

    D.   Friar, Reeve, Manciple, Man of Law

19. Which tales take place in the Orient?

    A.   The Wife of Bath's Tale and the Nun's Priest's Tale

    B.   The Prioress's Tale and the Knight's Tale

    C.   The Man of Law's Tale and the Squire's Tale

    D.   The Miller's Tale and the Clerk's Tale

20. Which pilgrim carries a brooch inscribed with Latin words meaning "Love Conquers All"?

    A.   The Prioress

    B.   The Wife of Bath

    C.   The Monk

    D.   The Squire

21. At what time of year does the pilgrimage take place?

    A.   In the dead of winter

    B.   In the height of spring

    C.   "That time of year when yellow leaves . . . hang upon these boughs"

    D.   On a midsummer night

22. Which characters are connected to the Church?

    A.   The Prioress, the Monk, the Friar, the Summoner, and the Pardoner

    B.   The Miller, the Ploughman, and the Reeve

    C.   The Knight, the Manciple, and the Host

    D.   The Canon's Yeoman, the Physician, the Clerk, and the Man of Law

23. Which tale is about a talking falcon?

   A. The Nun's Priest's Tale
   B. The Canon's Yeoman's Tale
   C. The Franklin's Tale
   D. The Squire's Tale

24. Which tales are about the patient suffering of women?

   A. The Wife of Bath's Tale and the Prioress's Tale
   B. The Knight's Tale, the Cook's Tale, and the Nun's
      Priest's Tale
   C. The Man of Law's Tale, the Clerk's Tale, and the
      Physician's Tale
   D. The Tale of Melibee, the Parson's Tale, and the
      Friar's Tale

25. Why does the Pardoner upset the Host?

   A. The Pardoner is homosexual.
   B. The Pardoner tries to sell indulgences to the pilgrims
      after he has already told them that he cheats people.
   C. The Pardoner has physically attacked the Host with
      his heavy bag of relics.
   D. The Pardoner refuses to give the Host an indulgence.

SUGGESTIONS FOR FURTHER READING

BLAMIRES, ALCUIN. *Chaucer, Ethics, and Gender.* Oxford, UK: Oxford University Press, 2006.

BROWN, PETER, ed. *A Companion to Chaucer.* Oxford, UK: Blackwell Publishers, reprint edition 2002.

CHAUCER, GEOFFREY. *The Riverside Chaucer.* Ed. Larry Benson. Boston: Houghton Mifflin, 1987.

COOPER, HELEN. *The Structure of* THE CANTERBURY TALES. London: Duckworth Press, 1983.

HOWARD, DONALD. *The Idea of* THE CANTERBURY TALES. Berkeley: University of California Press, 1976.

KNAPP, PEGGY A. *Chaucer and the Social Contest.* New York: Routledge, 1990.

PEARSALL, DEREK. *The Canterbury Tales.* London: G. Allen & Unwin, 1985, reprint edition 1993.

WETHERBEE, WINTHROP. *Chaucer:* THE CANTERBURY TALES. Cambridge, UK: Cambridge University Press, 2nd edition 2003.